YOU SAY
MORE
THAN YOU
THINK

YOU SAY
MORE
THAN YOU
THINK

The 7-Day Plan

for Using the

New Body Language

to Get What You Want

Janine Driver

with Mariska van Aalst

CROWN PUBLISHERS

New York

Published in the United States by Crown Publishers, an imprint of the Crown
Publishing Group, a division of Random House, Inc., New York

www.crownpublishing.com

Crown and the Crown colophon are registered trademarks of
Random House, Inc.

Library of Congress Cataloging-in-Publication Data

Driver, Janine.
You say more than you think : use the new body language to get what you
want!, the 7-day plan / Janine driver with Mariska van Aalst.—1st ed.
p. cm.
Includes bibliographical references.
ISBN 978-0-307-45937-6
1. Body language. 2. Self-confidence. 3. Communication.
I. Aalst, Mariska van. II. Title.
BF637.N66D75 2010
153.6'9—dc22   2009022344

ISBN 978-0-307-45397-6

Printed in the United States of America

Design by Nicola Ferguson

10 9 8 7 6 5 4 3 2 1

First Edition

To my mother, Lorraine Driver,
who is fighting breast cancer
with admirable perseverance,
resilience, and optimism.

CONTENTS

CONTENTS

Without Saying a Word, You Say More Than You Think

Mind not only what people say, but how they say it; and if you have any sagacity, you may discover more truth by your eyes than by your ears. People can say what they will, but they cannot look just as they will; and their looks frequently reveal what their words are calculated to conceal.

—LORD CHESTERFIELD (1694-1773), Letter to his Son

Imagine a mirror suddenly dropped down before you during your last meeting, sales negotiation, date, friendly get-together, or confrontation.

Would you be able to spot the subtle nonverbal clues that may be sabotaging you in these situations—and keeping you from reaching your fullest potential?

Are your facial expressions awkward?
Are your hand gestures not quite right?
Do you appear weak or arrogant or older than you are?
Does the way you shake hands discourage people from doing
   business with you?
Does your body language clash with your words?
Do you have a glaring flaw that *everyone notices but you?*

We interact with other people all day long, in every meaning-ful moment in our lives. But we don't always understand what they're thinking—nor do they understand our thoughts. If we don't have well-developed social perception, we may experience repeated failures: losing to the competition, job interview bombs, failed dates, trampled trust. But if we can hone that perception, learn to read people better, and communicate more effectively, that knowledge helps us in every part of our lives. We start to enjoy more exciting career opportunities, more honest friendships, better dating prospects, even more frequent wins at work!

Look at the successful people who cross your path daily. I'd bet most have at least two characteristics in common. First, they possess a sense of serene self-awareness. They seem comfortable in their own skin. Second, they have a better-than-average ability to connect with other people. They know how to put people at ease and create an immediate sense of rapport. Both of these traits stem directly from a strong com-mand of body language.

Uncovering the mysteries of body language—how people commu-nicate their thoughts and feelings without saying a word—is a power-ful first step toward mastering any social situation. All successful people know that the ability to detect and react to the split-second signals that skim across people's bodies hundreds of times each day is crucial to get-ting what they want in life. When something they're doing isn't effective, they've learned how to adjust their actions to maximize the moment.

Some people are gifted at body language—certain politicians or actors, for example, have a natural ability to woo others with their mere presence. Others try to emulate those lucky gifted few. They study their "tricks" and copy them, or they pore over body language textbooks to try to memorize individual signals to apply in certain situations.

This approach, unfortunately, has its risks. Authentic, effective body language is more than the sum of its parts. When people work from this rote-memory, dictionary approach, they stop seeing the bigger picture, all the diverse aspects of social perception. Instead, they see a person with crossed arms and think, "Reserved, angry." They see a smile and think, "Happy." They use a firm handshake to show other people "who is boss."

Easy, right?

Actually, I think they're making it hard, way harder than it needs to be.

Trying to use body language by reading a body language dictionary is like trying to speak French by reading a French dictionary. Things tend to fall apart in an inauthentic mess. Your actions seem robotic; your body language signals are disconnected from one another. You end up confusing the very people you're trying to attract because your body language just rings false. Your customers continue to be unsure of you. Your boss thinks you don't respect her. Your date thinks you hate him. Your lying teen just laughs at you.

That's why we need to move beyond the vacuum of disjointed, artificial body language to an approach based on *you*—your life, your history, your habits. An approach that builds your confidence from the outside in, one that keeps expanding your potential the longer you use it. But most of all, an approach that makes sense in your world, that applies in all situations, that feels natural and easy to use—because it is.

I've worked with more than fifty thousand people—from hardened cops to senior-level executives to pampered heiresses—to help them improve their body language, and I've come to believe one thing: we are *all* gifted in body language. Every single one of us has natural ability—we just need to learn how to tap into it. And once we do, the results can be life-changing:

- Employees have learned to hold their own in the boardroom and be treated well by the big boys.
- Those with social anxiety disorder have learned how to meet new people, more effectively manage their relationships, and build strong alliances.
- Middle-aged singles have gained the confidence to get back out in the dating scene.
- Women have learned how to read the judges in their divorce trials.
- "Alpha dogs" have discovered how to steady their nerves after a business downturn and get their power back.

- Others have discovered how to get the upper hand in negotiations so they're never again manipulated by a mechanic, car salesperson, or family member.
- And all have been taught how to know what to do when what they're doing isn't working.

Seeing these kinds of changes in the people I've worked with is what drove me to write this book and share this program with you. I want to help you—no matter how stuck or shy or socially awkward you are—to switch on the natural body language abilities that I *know* you already have.

This program has evolved over fifteen years of careful study, hundreds of seminars and training sessions, and way too many encounters with out-and-out liars. I've combined all of the tricks and techniques I've learned to bring out this natural ability into one integrated program. You don't have to comb the research or haul out the textbooks; I've done that for you. You can concentrate on creating the results you want. Because optimizing your body language isn't about studying or memorizing. It's about experiencing life.

Think of the way we learn to ride a bike, dance, or kiss. We use all of our experiences—our senses, gut instincts, some helpful "instruction," and a lot of practice. (Especially the kissing!) Once we've learned it, we know it; we can do it automatically, without thinking, because at some level, *we already knew how to do it.*

The 7-Day New Body Language program helps you mine your own experiences, senses, and gut instincts to develop your natural body language ability. No longer will you sabotage yourself unknowingly with negative nonverbal cues or bumble through life on the sidelines. You'll learn to trust your own natural instincts that tell you if someone is lying, in love with you, or a total loser. You'll learn to perfect your natural expressions, so you can appear more charming, caring, or cutthroat. Whatever *your* intentions, whatever *your* goals, the New Body Language plan starts with your habits at your comfort level and builds from there. Because, ultimately, the New Body Language program is all about creating **more confidence:**

- More confidence to read people (Accuracy);
- More confidence to use body language masterfully (Application); and
- More confidence to radiate your amazing self to the outside world (Attitude).

But why should you listen to me? Because these techniques not only saved my reputation—they saved my life.

Confidence Was My Weapon

I haven't always spent my days advising people on how to become better in business or ace job interviews or score hot dates. My career as an official body language expert started as a federal law enforcement officer for the Bureau of Alcohol, Tobacco, and Firearms and Explosives, ATF, for short.

I wish I could say getting that job was my lifelong childhood dream, but it wasn't. As fate would have it, my college career counselor referred me to an old friend who worked for the small law enforcement agency, which, until that point, I'd never even heard of. A few months later, when I told my dad I'd gotten a job with an agency called Alcohol, Tobacco, and Firearms and Explosives, he said, "I'm glad you could turn your hobbies into a career." (That dad of mine—always a jokester.)

In my early years with ATF, while still in the field, I was able to identify and decode the nonverbal cues of skinheads, nazis, and gun dealers who trafficked weapons to felons and teenagers, which allowed me to immediately adjust my approach and my body language to establish rapport and build trust quickly. I became known as someone who could easily detect if a person was lying or not. While I was in the thick of it, out in the field daily, I made the conscious connection between understanding body language and projecting confidence.

You may be saying to yourself, "Sure, it's easy to be confident when you have a badge, a nine millimeter strapped to your side, and the authority to throw someone in the slammer."

But I was an investigator, not a special agent. I didn't have a gun, and

I didn't have the authority to put someone in jail. Other than a badge, I didn't have any leverage. Yet, at the age of twenty-one, I was inspecting large explosives manufacturers and importers, dirty and dingy old pawnbroker shops, and going inside more than five hundred gun dealers' homes unannounced, some of whom sold machine guns. More often than not I was alone in the middle of nowhere, enforcing often controversial gun laws to a bunch of gun-toting, intimidating men—all before GPSs and cell phones. As you can imagine, as a representative of the U.S. government, I was never the most welcome guest.

My only weapon—and I carried it with me at all times—was confidence. The confidence that came from the ability to size people up quickly and understand much more about them in seven seconds than they ever would suspect. The confidence that came from using this knowledge to adjust my strategy in an instant. And the confidence that I had this secret weapon of body language awareness—but most of my suspects didn't.

By the age of twenty-four, my expertise at reading people landed me a slot as one of the bureau's youngest instructors. Over the next fifteen years, I taught interviewing and deception detection courses to new inspectors and special agent hires at the Federal Law Enforcement Training Center in Glynco, Georgia. By the age of thirty-one, I was teaching body language to more than thirty thousand law enforcement officers and U.S. attorneys across North America for the presidential initiative Project Safe Neighborhoods. I had the honor to work with some of the world's foremost experts on nonverbal communication, including my mentor, J. J. Newberry, retired ATF special agent and CEO of the Institute of Analytic Interviewing, aka the "Human Lie Detector"; Dr. Paul Ekman, an award-winning researcher into microexpressions and the seven universal emotions; and Dr. Mark Frank, a leading authority on behavioral observation.

These decades of experience in federal law enforcement and deception training taught me how to use body language to prevent disaster and bring the bad guys to justice. They also taught me that people can make mistakes. Sometimes big mistakes, often unintentional ones, but mistakes that leave them shaking their heads in confusion wondering, "What went wrong?"

Handle with Care

During those years at the ATF, I came to realize that reading and responding to body language is an awful lot like handling explosives. Used correctly, they can both be extraordinarily effective. But you have to stay aware—you never know when they're going to blow up in your face.

Ask yourself: Has there ever been a time in your life where you got so caught up in the moment that you didn't think through all the potential consequences of your actions? Maybe poor judgment cost you a missed business opportunity, your personal safety, a spouse, the love of one of your children, respect from colleagues, or even self-respect.

Now consider this: over 50 percent of what we communicate with others is nonverbal. If you aren't aware of the raw power of your body language, you are taking an unnecessary risk.

When you don't realize *You Say More Than You Think,* your personal, professional, and social life could blow up when you least expect it. And you'll be left with the scars of failure and defeat. Sound extreme? If you received a box of explosive chemicals and the wrapper said you had a 50/50 chance of getting hurt, wouldn't you do everything you could to minimize that risk? Or if you had a 50/50 chance of winning the lottery, wouldn't you buy a ticket? Wouldn't you agree that walking around not knowing how more than 50 percent of what you say influences others could be a big mistake?

I'm not saying these things to scare you, only to help you realize what's at stake. That's why I have so much confidence in this program. I know these techniques will work in your life, because I've used them in life-or-death situations. I've learned how to spot the most gifted liars on the planet. If I can use these techniques to persuade criminals to surrender, confess, and submit to prosecution—or even not to kill me—you can certainly use them to protect yourself while you're talking with your boss, customer, brother, or bratty kid.

Consider the New Body Language to be your Kevlar jacket and helmet. Just as I learned to read the signals in the faces and body movements of my suspects, you'll learn to interpret body language cues with a level of *Accuracy* that will keep you safe. Then, you'll learn how to react with the best *Application* of body language signals to get the outcome that *you* want. And most important, the combination of these two important facets will help you get the winning *Attitude,* the confidence to take command of any situation and influence it in your direction. You'll have the control and be able to change the dynamics of any interaction according to your needs and desires. You'll have the secret weapon—confidence—that all successful people share.

From Busting the Bad Guys to Helping the Good

In the fall of 2003, while still with the bureau, I created Lyin' Tamer Education (www.lyintamer.com), a leadership innovation company that combines up-to-date human potential research with body language to help individuals and corporations develop their executive presence and ultimately increase productivity and profitability. Thereafter, I opened the Body Language Institute (www.bodylanguageinstitute.com), located in Alexandria, Virginia, where people can get certified in Body Language and Detecting Deception, and become trainers in those two programs.

Since founding my first company I've shared these techniques with federal agencies like the FBI, CIA, Defense Intelligence Agency; Fortune 500 companies like AOL, Coca-Cola, Hard Rock hotels, *Cosmopolitan* magazine, Lockheed Martin, and Accenture; as well as with millions of viewers of national television from *The Rachael Ray Show* to NBC's *Today* to CNN's *Larry King Live.* I've seen how the most powerful techniques I'd learned with the bureau could help out everyday men and women, people who struggled with the same faults in confidence despite very different life circumstances. Think about this . . .

How much money would you save your company if you knew the truth behind a job applicant's résumé, or if you knew what your employee's strengths and weaknesses were, before having to spend thousands of dollars on training so he or she could leave your company and work for your competitor a year later?

How much time would you save if you were able to detect if a particular salesperson was open to negotiating?

How many tears could you spare yourself (and lives could you save) if you really knew your kid was telling you the truth when you asked him, "Are you doing drugs?"

That's what this plan can do for you—help you read any situation with accuracy, determine the best body language application, and transmit the attitude that keeps *you* in control.

My Promise to You

This book will help you grasp the essentials of how to use the New Body Language to get what you want. You'll learn to strengthen interpersonal relationships, become a stronger leader, manage your nerves better, and attain ambitious new goals. You'll be better prepared to perform as a persuasive communicator, problem solver, and cunning negotiator. With your pumped-up confidence and enthusiasm, you'll save time, money, resources, and gain that all-important edge in an often challenging global environment.

To get started, we'll blast seven established myths of the Old Body Language that may have been holding you back. In their place, we'll explore the flexibility, versatility, and resilience of the New Body Language and how the 7-Day program will help you develop your natural social ability in a way that's so much richer than the sum of its parts. Then, starting from Day 1, we'll go day by day through the week's lesson plan, each day sharing several stories, exercises, and techniques that will reach down and tap that innate ability, helping you refine and perfect your accuracy when reading body language and your application when executing body language.

Each day you'll also discover several 7-Second Fixes that pick up on that chapter's themes, suggestions you can implement immediately to help you effortlessly enhance your relationships with others. At the end of the week, we'll put it all together in one easy-to-remember process that you can automatically use each time you're in a body-reading situation.

As you move through the program, you'll hear inspiring first-person accounts from several of my former students, all members of a Body Language Power Team who'd previously struggled with ineffective body language that had held them back for years. After following the program in this book for one week, they were able to launch businesses, find new love, expand their social circles, discover hidden talents—in other words, make things happen!

THE MAKING OF THE
BODY LANGUAGE POWER TEAM

In the spring of 2007, *The Rachael Ray Show* contacted me to be an undercover body language expert. My mission: to give two women who were being held back in their lives a twelve-hour body language makeover.

Fast-forward one month and Nicole, who'd previously been unlucky in love, was in a very promising relationship. Julianne, who'd been frustrated with her stagnant career, had landed her dream job as a designer at Tommy Hilfiger.

Nicole and Julianne's success not only helped inspire me to write this book but also to create a Body Language Power Team (BLPT). As you go through the book, you'll hear stories from members of my BLPT, a group of people who've completed this program. In each chapter, you'll meet a person who'd previously struggled with certain body signals, but who used these exercises to make a tremendous change in his or her life. ○

To watch video clips, to meet all the original BLPT participants, to read their blogs, or to share your own success story, visit www.yousaymorethanyouthink.com.

Bottom line: if I could use these techniques to outsmart gun-runners and white-collar criminals, you can certainly use them to discipline your teen, score a hot date, or get that long sought-after promotion. In just one week, you'll tap into your natural ability to read others accurately, apply body language appropriately, and earn a kick-ass attitude that will affect all areas of your life. From that first date to the one hundredth, from the pushy car salesman to the passive-aggressive "frenemy," learning the New Body Language will help you get what you need out of any kind of relationship.

Ready for this? You bet you are. Let's go!

The New Body Language: *What I'll Tell You That Other Experts Won't*

ONE

> If language was given to men to conceal
> their thoughts, then gesture's purpose
> was to disclose them.
> —*JOHN NAPIER (1550-1617)*, Hands

One afternoon, after a deadly shoot-out at a Richmond, California, hamburger stand, a young woman was found cowering under a car. The woman turned out to be a terrified cousin of the recently deceased. She told the investigator she'd greeted her cousin with a quick, "Hey, cuz," at the hamburger stand and started to walk around the building to go to the bathroom. Then she'd heard a loud noise and immediately dove under a car for refuge. Did you see the shooter? the investigator wondered. No, she said, I'm sorry, but I didn't see who shot my cousin.

The investigator suspected that there was more to the story, so he brought in J. J. Newberry, Truth Wizard. (No, really—that's actually his title. A Truth Wizard is a person who's been scientifically proven to detect lies accurately at least 80 percent of the time. As the number one human lie detector in the world, J. J.'s rate is *over 90 percent*.)

The stakes were high. The suspect, One-Eyed Marvin, was a known drug dealer who'd been terrorizing the area with drive-by shootings, pipe bombings, and targeted hits on competing cocaine dealers—and their children, innocent bystanders, or anyone unfortunate enough to witness his crimes.

J. J. walked into the interview room very deliberately. He gave the young woman a firm handshake, then faced her directly but with a laid-back demeanor. He started with some small talk, to make her feel at ease. While he maintained an open pose, he asked a lot of questions, listening with his ears and, even more important, with his eyes.

After establishing rapport, J. J. asked the young woman to explain what happened the night of the incident. She repeated the same story she had told the first investigator:

"I said hello to my cousin who was at the hamburger stand and walked toward the corner of the building to go the bathroom. I heard a loud sound. I dove under a car to hide. And that's where the police found me, just ask them."

J. J. didn't interrupt her or finish her sentences. He simply let her speak. When she was done, J. J. used a friendly but curious voice. "I've been to that hamburger stand," he said. "And there's no bathroom behind there."

"No, I went back there to squat down," she replied. "Everyone does it."

J. J. had, of course, already known that people went behind that building to do their business; he wanted to see if she would tell him the truth. J. J. was analyzing her baseline behavior: her tone of voice, rhythm of speaking, hand gestures, stance, and posture. Any time that she deviated from her normal behavior, he could ask her specific open-ended questions to get her to reveal the truth. At that point J. J. asked her an odd question: "Did you sense a pending fear of danger?"

"What?" she asked, confused.

J. J. repeated the question. "When you saw your cousin at the hamburger stand, did you sense a pending fear of danger?"

She confidently responded, "No, not at all."

J. J. stood up. "Okay, that's all I wanted to know." But while making his way out of the room, J. J. abruptly pounded his fist on the desk behind the young woman. She immediately whipped her head around, toward the sound, to see what was going on.

Just as Colombo himself would have done, J. J. looked right at her and said, "See what you just did? You turned your head toward the sound to see if you were in any kind of danger. Everyone who hears an unexpected burst of sound instinctively looks to see where it's coming from, in order to know if they are in imminent danger. Then they determine where to run."

He looked her even more directly in the eye. "And just as you turned to look at me, you looked toward your cousin when he was shot, and you saw the shooter, didn't you?"

Immediately the young woman burst into tears. "Yes . . . yes, I did," she whimpered. "One-Eyed Marvin killed my cousin . . . with a machine gun."

J. J. moved toward her and immediately hugged his new witness. "It's okay. I know you're afraid, but it's okay. We'll take care of you. Just tell us the truth."

J. J. Newberry's primary secret ingredient during that interview, and every interview he does, is confidence. He has tapped so thoroughly into his innate body language skills that he knows how to establish rapport with anyone. When you have that kind of easy, comfortable rapport with people, they let down their guard. You can see how they really think and how they really react, so you can adjust your body language to their unconscious preferences. Just like that, they'll start to trust you automatically.

J. J. uses this process to convince people to just tell the truth. You can use this process in much the same way—to get to the bottom of any story, to stay in control of any situation, even to influence people to do what you'd like them to do. You'll start with your own instincts and strengthen them with the strategies in this book. You'll develop an entire repertoire of skills to respond to any situation and subtly retain the upper hand, no matter which way things go.

What you will *not* do is memorize a series of positions and gestures. The New Body Language is so much richer than that.

7 Myths of the Old Body Language

Now, what would have happened had J. J. gone into that interrogation room like a car salesman at the end of the fiscal year, eager to make the next sale? Maybe his mug plastered with a fake grin, manic energy level, overly firm handshake, intense eye contact, speaking quickly, maybe even steepling his hands (a notorious hand gesture for "powerful people")?

I'll tell you what would have happened: he would have looked desperate and insincere, and most likely would have destroyed his credibility.

While all of these signals are on the Old Body Language list of powerful or influential signals, none of them would help him in this situation. J. J. knew he would be better served if he telegraphed empathy and self-confidence by using relaxed facial expressions, little body movement, fewer gestures, and a slower and lower manner of speaking. Yet during job interviews, sales negotiations, and first dates from Los Angeles to New York City, would-be successful leaders make this colossal mistake every day. Flipping through a compendium of body language, they've mixed up their own little concoction of "success" signals: a wide stance here, a dash of power gestures there, a brief touch here, and a full cup of eye contact there. But what they don't realize is that the clustering of too many power gestures at once, or even one wrong move used at the wrong time, will likely harm, if not ruin, your chances for your desired outcome.

Has this ever happened to you? Have you thought you knew something about body language but somehow you sabotaged your success, either with subconscious messages you sent to others or by misinterpreting another person's signals?

If so, you're not alone. That's one of the primary reasons I wrote this book—to help people learn how to *integrate* their interpretation and execution of body language signals, so they all come together in a seamless, natural, fluid way, without resorting to any of the awkward robotics of the Old Body Language. The "insert signal A into situation B" approach is not effective—this myth gets a lot of press but, unfortunately, it's not true. And it's only one of several Old Body Language myths.

Myth #1: *Reading body language signals can help you read minds.* If you've watched TV lately, or opened up a celebrity magazine in the last five years, you've no doubt been bombarded with split-second body language analysis of political figures, pop stars, even little kids. Listening to these analyses, you might be convinced there are absolute meanings behind every move we make—that all you have to do is simply learn to interpret a handful of body language signals and you, too, can be a mind reader.

This makes my bullsh*t detector go insane. I have a rule that anytime I do a body language analysis of a photograph, I have to see a minimum of twenty other images of the person. That's the only way I can see if his behavior is unusual and telling or if it is entirely normal for him. I never say, "This body language signal means . . ." I always say, "It could be *perceived as* this." Because every body language "rule" has exceptions.

For example, on August 28, 1963, during the civil rights rally on the steps at the Lincoln Memorial in Washington, D.C., Dr. Martin Luther King Jr. gave his "I Have a Dream" speech. And had you been one of the quarter-million people in attendance that day, and you were watching for specific body language signals, you might have thought that, no, he did *not* have a dream. After all, Dr. King shook his head from left to right throughout the speech, didn't he?

See the problem?

Yes, the scientific community has racked up a ton of research that proves nonverbal communication speaks louder than our words. But no, the definitive meanings we put on gestures have not yet been proven. That's the biggest misperception that fuels the Old Body Language. Because the truth is the individual signals themselves do not mean what we want them to mean; they're defined by how others perceive them, and then react to them.

For example, if you're in a 3:00 P.M. meeting with your boss, and he wrinkles his nose, you might read that as a microexpression of disgust and think, "I knew it! He doesn't like what I just said." In fact, he might just be thinking about the mess his new puppy is going to leave in his house if he has to work late again. If you're operating from the Old Body Language model, you might fall into a panic, reading that sign as a clue that you're about to be laid off. And, oh gosh, you'll lose your health insurance . . . and maybe even your home!

Calm down, skipper. You're not a mind reader. You can't be—at least not based on one single signal. You have to have more to work with than that.

Myth #2: *You can use individual signals to cover up your true feelings.* This is the flip side to Myth #1. Simple answer? No, you can't. No one signal tells the whole story, whether you're interpreting the signals or delivering them.

Let's say you're terrified to ask a woman on a date, but decide to grit your teeth and do it—as she is, after all, quite a hottie. To convince her you're a confident, strong man, you'll use a forward pickup line and a quick wink—yeah, that's it!—and hope she won't notice your gripped, sweaty fists. And does that work for you?

I'm guessing not so well. Your message comes from the whole package, not just one planned signal. If your wink is saying, "Hey, baby," and the rest of your body is screaming, "Eek, you scare me!" you'll probably confuse her. Whereas she might have thought your authentic shyness a bit endearing, your odd mix of conflicting signals will break rapport and trust, and probably kill all chances of success.

Myth #3: *Certain power gestures, like the steeple, will make people respect you.* Speaking coaches will often advise people to use the steepling gesture (fingertips to fingertips, like prayer hands) to convey power. For people who want to get more respect in their daily lives, this kind of Old Body Language suggestion can seem like the quick fix they've been searching for.

Again, a total myth. As a matter of fact, on a first date, a steeple would be a romance killer. And if someone is pouring her heart out to you, steepling would shut her down and break rapport—she would probably see you as a self-centered jerk.

Steepling isn't the only power signal rife with risks. Who can forget the 2000 presidential debates, when Al Gore walked into George W. Bush's personal space while Bush was still speaking? What Gore may have thought was a confident, powerful move—commanding more of the physical space—just made him come off as a bully.

Bottom line: there are no one-size-fits-all gestures. Signals that work in some situations could be lethal in others. So unless you're a Donald Trump, and people expect that kind of endearing dominance from you every second, approach power gestures with caution. Using them at the wrong time won't help your cause—you'll only come across as cocky and arrogant.

Myth #4: *All body language is universal.* Big no-no. True, nonverbal communication pioneer Paul Ekman did prove that all humans show similar facial signals for each of seven universal emotions—anger, contempt, disgust, fear, happiness, sadness, and surprise. But beyond that, almost every other body language signal, from the way we use our heads (some cultures nod to say yes; others, like in Bulgaria, shake them) to the way we use our feet (some cultures see the foot as an erogenous zone; others, as the most offensive part of the body), is completely dependent on who raised you, where, and how. Dangers of misinterpretation lurk around every distant corner, so definitely leave your Old Body Language textbook at home when you hit the road.

Myth #5: *Liars don't make eye contact.* Ah, one of the original Old Body Language myths. Were this but true! Then we wouldn't need extensive training, polygraphs, or other fancy tests. We wouldn't need J. J. and his expertise. No, sadly, liars are usually experts at maintaining eye contact. If anything, they tend to give a bit of extra eye contact: "I swear I'm telling you the truth—I'm looking you in the eye, aren't I?"

Instead of looking for stereotypical darting eyes and evasive glances, you should be looking for any change from a person's normal behavior. If a person goes from looking at you half the time, and drops down to 30 percent eye contact, okay. You might have a liar. Or if he or she goes from 50 percent eye contact to 90 percent—yeah, you might have busted the person on that one. But don't make the mistake of looking for evasive eyes, or you may be convinced the world's most honest-but-shy person is a total bald-faced liar.

Myth #6: *Our eyes go up and to the right when we are withholding the truth or making up a story.* This is one of those Old Body Language pseudoscientific myths that got its start from the study of neurolinguistic programming (NLP). The theory has been proven incorrect, but it's a myth that continues to be told again and again and has exploded almost overnight like office gossip. Although most people do look to their upper right when creating an answer, we don't know if the answer will be a fabrication or simply a well-processed answer. For instance, if I said, "What was the favorite gift you got for your birthday?" you may look to the upper right because you suddenly think about the fact that *next year* you turn forty. You don't verbally mention your fear of turning forty, but your eye movements trigger a false positive that you are lying and fabricating your answer when you tell me what your favorite gift was.

Myth #7: *Smile at everyone you meet—people will respect you for it.* This Old Body Language myth seems like just plain common sense, right? Kind of along the same lines as "Treat others as you'd like to be treated" or "Laugh and the world laughs with you." But studies have shown that people who smile more often are actually seen as having less status and less power than those who smile only occasionally. In other words, betas smile, alphas don't.

On the other hand, we know from the latest neuroscience research that our brains are programmed to "catch" the other person's delight and happiness whenever we see a genuine smile. So the New Body Language approach is to combine the two: wait until you've been introduced, then as you shake your new acquaintance's hand and say her name, you smile broadly. Body-language-savvy alpha leaders know this trick—it's as if you and your name brought a smile to their face. Sneaky, huh? But the effect can feel very genuine.

The New Body Language:
Accuracy + Application = Attitude

Why does anyone pick up a book on body language? Why did you? In my experience, people are usually interested in studying body language for one of two reasons:

a. You believe you are more shy or socially awkward than the average person, and you think that the way you interact with people may be holding you back. You're looking for some suggestions to make yourself look more natural and effortless when you're among people you don't know that well.

b. You think you're already pretty good at socializing and psyching people out, but you want to learn to do it better, so you can get an even bigger edge. You want to learn more "tricks" and insider information, so you can use your body language to convince others to do what you want.

Now, you might see these as opposite ends of the spectrum. But really what both of these people are looking for is more *confidence*. And that's what the New Body Language is all about—creating the authentic confidence that comes when you know how to read people better (accuracy) and automatically put your best foot forward (application). When you have New Body Language confidence, the "right" body language interpretations and moves come to you effortlessly, in the moment, and you don't have to think about them anymore.

In my experience, these two aspects break down by gender. Many women can *read* body language extremely well, but may have trouble projecting even basic signals of confidence. Many men can *project* that ultra-confidence (some more successfully than others), but don't realize that reading body language comes first. The New Body Language is about integrating *both*—only then will you gain authentic confidence, the attitude that will help you get the most out of this program, and out of life!

At the end of this chapter, you'll take a quiz to determine your current Body Language Confidence Quotient, so you can see where to place yourself on the continuum, and determine where your greatest accuracy and application strengths and challenges lie. Perhaps you're a master at observation, but fall down on execution. Perhaps you pride yourself on your smooth moves, but aren't reading others' signs very well. Whatever your particular concern, we'll sort it out. At the end of the week, no matter where you are today, you'll have the attitude that will give you the power to master any situation.

But first, let's take a closer look at some key aspects of this three-phase approach.

Phase 1: Read Others with ACCURACY

The first phase in New Body Language is, by necessity, accuracy: you have to learn to read your situation and your target well—without being distracted or biased—to respond with the proper body language application. Misread the situation, blow the response. Blow the response, and you'll have to work twice as hard to regain your lost footing.

As you've no doubt sensed, based on J. J.'s experience, my training, and the hundreds of new studies published every year about nonverbal behavior—accuracy is tricky! Let's talk about a few key concepts that help reveal why true accuracy is so complex—and why it's worth the effort.

Trust the Visual Information Channel

The Visual Information Channel is simply all the information you receive with your eyes as opposed to your ears. Occasionally during my corporate body language classes, I'll do an exercise students say is very entertaining, which shows how important the Visual Information Channel is. I have half the class watch an episode of the perfect body language cartoon, *Tom & Jerry*, while the other half of the class leaves the room. When it's over, the portion of the class that was in the hall returns and interviews the people who saw the short cartoon clip. The catch? The people who watched the cartoon must describe the entire episode without using hand and arm gestures—they have to sit on their hands.

This exercise is so challenging that some people squirm under the pressure of their hands moving around beneath them. Some simply cannot communicate the story line without using their hands.

The point of this exercise is to prove how uncomfortable and difficult it is for people *not* to use their hands and arms when they talk, to show exactly how essential the Visual Information Channel is to communication. We use hand gestures in most areas of speech, especially to help us express information that is difficult to get across with words alone. Just try to give a driver directions to the local hospital, or explain how to climb a ladder, or try to describe a football, without using your hands—not impossible, but extremely difficult and unnatural feeling.

Gestures are so intricately linked to speech that they even shape the way we learn to speak and to process information. One study from the University of Chicago found that children who used gestures when they explained how to solve math problems performed better and mastered more diverse math strategies than kids who didn't.

Gestures also help the listener. Researchers found that when parents of fourteen-month-old babies used gestures more often ("Timmy, do you see this book?" [pointing to a book]), their kids not only used more gestures themselves, they also had more advanced vocabularies when they were four and a half.

The key is that a person's gestures must match his words, or the brain of the person listening might actually stumble for a brief moment. Neuroscientist Spencer Kelly of Colgate University conducted a study in which he measured how the brain responds when a person witnesses different combinations of gestures and words. Dr. Kelly found that when we hear someone speak words that do not match her gestures—such as, "You have to go around to the left," while you point to the right—the brain experiences a brief hiccup. The study revealed that the subjects' brain waves were radically altered, slowing down activity, suggesting that the brain tends to process the meaning of the gesture with the meaning of the spoken word—and when they're mismatched, comprehension as a whole suffers.

So how do you think you would feel as the person who is watching those mismatched gestures? Likely you'd have that "Huh?" sensation, that feeling you get when you're not sure you understand what a person is saying. At that moment, because you're a polite person, you'd probably try to force yourself to pay closer attention to the speaker's words—you'd tell yourself, "Maybe I'm just missing something."

But no! You are most definitely *not* missing something. That brain hiccup is actually a gift; it is part of your intuitive body language sense that something is wrong. Something about the person is not quite genuine.

The trick is to recognize when that brain hiccup is happening and to trust your instincts. You've taken an important step to accurately assess the situation: using the Visual Information Channel you've recognized that the person's body language is *incongruent,* or mismatched with the content of her speech. The New Body Language program helps you tune into that instinct, so you can recognize when you feel it, rather than dismiss it like the kind, polite person you are.

Inattentive Blindness

Have you ever been so focused on one goal that you missed what's right in front of your eyes? Have you ever gone to work on a Monday and had a coworker say to you, "Hey, I waved to you at the movies yesterday, you were three feet away, and you ignored me!"? Has your spouse ever said, "I thought you said my shoes were in the kitchen" when he had just stepped over them in the hallway?

When we focus simply on the trees, instead of taking the time to slow down our judgments and look at the entire forest, we can miss valuable information. This is a phenomenon called *inattentive blindness,* also known as *perceptual blindness,* and it's related to how our minds see and process information.

Each year, an eighteen-wheeler truck driver will look to his left before changing lanes, look directly at the person who is driving a motorcycle in that lane, and then pull into that lane anyway. And every summer a lifeguard somewhere who is constantly looking at a crystal-clear pool, will miss a young child who has already drowned because the child is at the bottom of the pool. The truck driver is looking for a car, not a motorcycle. And the lifeguard is looking for someone panicking and splashing at the surface of the pool, not someone at the bottom.

Much in the way that the ATF taught me to quickly assess any potentially dangerous situation quickly, the New Body Language program will help you develop your ability to quickly take in and analyze all the data in any given environment. As you work through the program, you'll strengthen your innate skills and instincts to pinpoint the key details that give you the critical information about any situation, environment, or interpersonal dynamic in which you may find yourself.

To gauge your own degree of inattentive blindness, I want you to take Part 1 of the "Test Your Inattentive Blindness" quiz that follows. After this test, you'll understand how our dulled perceptual habits can blind us to key details about nonverbal communication. When you're done, turn to page 25 for Part 2. No peeking! (Also, go to yousaymore thanyouthink.com and click on "Break the Code," then spot the differences between Pictures A and B.)

TEST YOUR INATTENTIVE BLINDNESS: PART 1

Set the timer for 30 seconds. Stand in the doorway of your bedroom and look at the ten largest objects in your room. When the timer goes off, leave the bedroom. Do you have your mental list? Turn to page 25 to complete Part 2 of the test. (Spoiler Alert—be sure to complete A before peeking at B and C; otherwise it won't work.) ○

Message Clusters

Both my mom (a nurse) and my dad (a mechanic) hold jobs that require looking not only at the smallest minute detail, but also at the big picture. Whether a patient's face is turning red or a car makes a clicking sound under the hood, both nurses and mechanics need to look for other symptoms to make an accurate assessment. They are constantly challenged to use multiple signals to "diagnose" any issue.

The same holds true in the New Body Language. You know you need more than one signal to make an accurate assessment. From now on, instead of decoding a person's intentions based on a dictionary-style definition of body language signals, you are going to look for *message clusters.*

All messages come in clusters that include posture, gestures, facial expressions, tone of voice, and more. Only by taking them all in and considering them as a unit, a single message cluster, will you get an accurate gauge of the person's potential feelings and thoughts. Grouping messages also helps you see those incongruent signals more easily, because they'll stick out like a sore thumb. (Remember that song? "One of these things is not like the other . . .")

Well-honed accuracy is the first step toward application, as you need to take in all available information about your target's signals to respond effectively. Next, let's take a look at application.

7-SECOND FIX

On a Date

The Problem: These baby boomers are out on a date and the smitten man doesn't know what to do with his hands or his body position. (You may have felt this way during a meeting or a job interview.) In the photo on the left, he sits directly across from his date, but his clasped hands make him appear nervous.

The Fix: Ladies, instead of sitting directly across from your date, sit off to the side and give your new man some space—but angle your belly button toward him and use open-palm gestures (which is often perceived as showing sincerity). Notice now that all three of his power zones (his belly button, naughty bits [we'll talk about this later], and neck) are all open. Follow her lead and he'll be confident like a tiger.

Phase 2: APPLY What You're Learning

Most people who attend my seminars have entrenched body language habits; we all do. But some are quite stubborn about changing them. They feel more comfortable, less self-conscious, when they do things a certain way. "I can't shake hands that way," they say. "It doesn't feel 'like me.'"

I can respect that. Not that I believe you "can't" do something, of course—you can do anything you set your mind to do. Recognizing that you have an instinctive body language pattern is very insightful, both about yourself and human beings in general. But that doesn't mean you can't control it.

TEST YOUR INATTENTIVE BLINDNESS: PART 2

First, do Part 1 of the test on page 23. Now, write down the ten *smallest* objects in your room.

Ha—Tricked you! I asked you to focus on the ten largest objects, but I actually want you to write down the ten smallest objects.

Now, go back to your room and see if your answers are correct. Could you name the ten smallest things in your room? Now sit on the floor and look around. Do you notice something that you didn't notice before?

If you missed something, blame your inattentive blindness—you didn't notice what was right in front of your eyes. Remember this exercise over the next seven days; use it as a reminder to look at your life and your interactions with others literally from a different perspective. ○

Hardwired Instincts

Many body language signals are hardwired. We've spoken briefly about Ekman's seven universal emotions, which show us that certain facial expressions of emotion are dictated entirely by our biology. Researchers continue to find evidence that other signals are biologically driven as well. In one fascinating study, scientists from the University of British Columbia observed athletes at the Olympic and Paralympic Games of 2004 to see how they would react to winning and losing. With 140 athletes from thirty-seven countries, they had a great cross section of humanity to consider. The researchers found that no matter where the athletes came from, winners would display similar reactions—they'd hold their heads back, punch the air with their fists, and puff out their chests. In contrast, losers would shrink, slouching their heads with their shoulders down.

You might think: *So what?* Everyone has seen television broadcasts of winners, receivers spiking balls in the end zone, soccer players ripping off their shirts after a goal. Everyone knows what a winner looks like.

Yeah, except if you're blind—which fifty-three of these athletes were.

Rewired Instincts

Some aspects of body language are intuitive and automatic. No question. But the number that are beyond our control are a tiny fraction of those signals we *can* control.

We have tremendous room for improvement and mastery. Just as you can learn to dance, or kiss, or ride a bike, you can learn to control the application of many aspects of your body language. That doesn't make you a self-involved phony. By perfecting your control, you may actually help other people feel better, too.

Take, for example, fear. We are all scared sometimes. Is it good for your career (or your love life) to show that fear to the world? To let it all hang out? To "be who you are," because anything else would be "dishonest"?

No. That would not be good. Fear is contagious, and no one likes to feel scared. Researchers believe when we look at someone experiencing a certain emotion (happiness, sadness, fear) or doing a certain action (yawning, smiling), specific brain cells called "mirror neurons" stimulate us to experience the same emotion or action. So when a job interviewer sees a look of fear on her applicant's face, she will feel a corresponding sense of fear as well—and she may want to create distance from you. That's why training yourself to project more confidence than you feel is always in your best interest. If you want others to feel confident about you, you have to make them feel that confidence, too.

For some, practicing confident body language will only feel uncomfortable the first few times, while for others, it will be easy sailing from the get-go. After that, the more you visualize and actually use confident body language, the quicker your body and brain will adjust and both will begin to believe—even if you still have your doubts. The day before and morning of an interview, visualize yourself being confident during the interview and it won't seem awkward during your face-to-face meeting. Fake it 'til you make it, baby.

Our brains are amazingly resilient, changeable organs. Neuroscience research has proven that repetition builds faith in our own abilities, the foundation for profound levels of mastery. Repetition signals our brain, "Hey there, gorgeous, you might want to hang on to this information." The more you repeat the key concepts in this book, the more they will make sense. Repetition ensures that this new information becomes a part of your brain's neural pathways and associations, and it makes you more likely to continue to use the information as well. As you step into this positive feedback loop of repetition/confidence/mastery/repetition, you'll quickly move toward a more natural, effortless use of body language.

I understand that sometimes a task may seem too large or too daunting to accomplish all at once. You won't turn into a body language master by tomorrow. But within a week's time, you can make a tremendous change. All it takes is absorbing some fundamental concepts, bit by bit.

Think about how kids learn baseball. The process that begins with learning how to put on a glove and not blink when you swing a bat could eventually lead to cracking a game-winning grand-slam home run—but you certainly couldn't do it the first day of Little League. The best way to learn is to start with the fundamentals, tap into your natural instincts, and build on each, practicing again and again over time. That's the only way true mastery can be achieved, when it all comes together in a seamless package of information rather than a large chunk of discon-nected facts you might not understand.

In each of the chapters in the book, I will break down a certain facet of the New Body Language into smaller components that build upon one another. The more you practice deciphering body language (accu-racy), and the more quality time you put into your practice (application), the more your brain pathways change, and the more confident you'll become (attitude).

Phase 3: Get the Right ATTITUDE

Once you've hit this stage, you'll see how it all ties together. Because the brain uses past learning as the guide for what to expect in the future, you'll soon know what is most likely to happen a second or two before things occur, and you'll immediately engage the success formulas in this book to get you what you want.

The world is thirsty for confident, but likable leaders. Leaders who can help effectively and profitably steer a company in the right direction and who can build customer loyalty and commitment.

That's why despite the challenging economy, I'm always on the road training associates, senior associates, managers, and even upper manage-ment on the softer skills, such as how they can not only appear, but ac-tually become more approachable, more sociable, and more open—how they can develop attitude.

Attitude is both a means to an end and the end we're all striving for. We all want to get that serene sense of security, that inner knowledge that we fully understand what people are thinking and we're able to in-fluence that thinking. Not to duplicitous ends, mind you—I firmly be-lieve that no matter what your intention, if it is to hurt someone, you will inevitably be hurt yourself. No, what I'm talking about is a less easily defined yet way more valuable special *something*.

Some of us are lucky—we're born with an effortless way of interact-ing with other people. Natural charm, you might call it. Or charisma. But many of us need to work to uncover this natural charm within our-selves. And if you put in one week's worth of work, you will.

The New Body Language 7-Day Plan

Over the past decade, I have hunted down all the proven formulas and strategies for maximizing body language and building self-confidence across any situation that I could think up. I tried them out first on my sisters, coworkers, parents, and friends. When they were successful, I taught them to my students. Then, I began to share choice tidbits with millions of viewers and listeners on shows like *Today, Rachael Ray, FOX News, Larry King Live,* and *Oprah & Friends* XM Radio. Through all this trial and error, seeing the before-and-after effects on thousands of people, I collected only those techniques and exercises that yielded the most dramatic results, the ones that really made a difference in people's lives, helped them reach those "Aha!" moments that can change everything. Out of those strategies came this progressive program. When you complete it this week, you'll have all the skills and confidence you need to use body language to get what you want in life.

What I'm going to say next will come as no surprise to any teachers out there: throughout my entire history as a trainer and instructor, I have noticed that the people who enjoyed the biggest breakthroughs were the ones who performed the exercise tasks I "prescribed" for them.

Huh, go figure. Homework does work.

By observing others closely, my students and clients were able to master the basics quickly, then move on to customize their approach with the exercises or techniques that worked best for them. By taking the time to learn how to keep their eyes on the ball, they eventually hit those home runs.

Consider this your spring training. Do the work, and the win will be yours.

Before the Big Day: How to Prepare for Your Week

I've broken this entire program down into small, doable, concrete steps. To get the results you want, you need to commit to completing all seven days consecutively, no more, no less. The exercises are fun, and they work. But to start off on the best foot, you'll need to do a few things.

1. Plan Your Schedule. For each of the days, schedule a half hour to three-quarters of an hour in the morning to read that day's chapter without interruption. Then block out at least an hour later that day to practice your newfound decoding skills. At the end of each chapter, you'll find practical exercises that anyone can use. If you're an indoor person, I have exercises that you can do on your computer while snuggled up in your PJs. And if you're a hands-on, get-out-there-and-interact kind of person, I've got what you need, too. I recommend that you use a combination of both types of exercises to get the best results. When you read and do your daily lesson is up to you; you just have to make sure to do both for seven consecutive days.

2. Create a Success Journal. Get a notebook or legal pad, whatever feels most comfortable to you. On the first page, write down your plan, which should include your preset reading and action hours. Also write out your answers to these questions I posed to the Body Language Power Teams that I facilitate around the country:

1. How would you describe yourself?
2. How would three different people in your life describe you?
3. What do you want?
4. What steps have you taken so far to get what you want?
5. What's stopping you right now?
6. Why do you think a body language makeover can help you?
7. What might stop you from completing all seven days of the program?
8. What will you do today to prevent yourself from being stopped?

Then, on its own page, write out and complete this sentence: "Better body language will help me _____."

Keep your answer short. For example, you might write "increase my sales," or "get a promotion," or "find my true love," or "connect with my friends and family." This sentence will be your mantra for the duration of the program. Knowing why you are here will help you recommit each day.

Your journal will be a place to record your thoughts and experiences throughout the week. When you've completed the program, the journal will also be a very good reminder of where you began and how your outlook on yourself and others changed after the program.

3. Get Your Siblings' Perspective. Choose three words to describe each of your parents. Now call one of your siblings or a family friend who knows (or knew) your parents well, and ask them to describe each one in three words. Were the answers different? Why? How can this new discovery shape the way you look at the week ahead? Or at life in general?

4. Create Your Baseline Videotape. Trust me, this is the best part! You will not believe how instructive this tool will be. If you're feeling shy or nervous, don't sweat it; the footage that you'll tape is for your eyes only. And if you don't have a video camera, borrow one. *Complete this step*—it's essential.

Point the camera at a chair, sit down, and talk about:

Your positive expectations of this program
How you'll know when you have gotten what you want
How your life will be different

A few *very important* videotaping rules:

1. Do not stop the tape and start over; first impressions have no second chances.
2. As tempting as it might be, *DO NOT* watch the videotape after you make it. You will do this later in the program when you'll be astonished by how well you'll be able to identify the ways that your body language was giving away your power.

5. Take the "BQ" Quiz. Answer the questions to the quiz that follows. Then enter your score and your profile. Take the results of this profile lightly; you'll revisit it at the end of the program.

Quiz: What's Your Body Language Confidence Quotient (BQ)?

How loudly does your body language convey confidence? Let's find out.

Pick one answer that is closest to what you might do, then total up your As, Bs, and Cs and when you're ready to discover your confidence quotient, turn the page.

	Questions	A	B	C
1	Distance between feet when standing	10 inches to 3 feet	6 inches to 10 inches	6 inches and under
2	Leg position when seated	Legs crossed/ankle over knee	Both feet planted on ground	Feet close together or crossed at ankles
3	Head/neck position	Head tilted back, neck exposed	Head level	Head tilted forward, throat hidden
4	Shoulder position	Pulled back (puffing out chest)	Relaxed	Slightly slumped forward
5	When shaking hands, your hand . . .	Comes in at an angle palm facing down	Is positioned vertically	Comes in at an angle palm facing up
6	When nervous, your hands are . . .	Behind your back or on your hips	Relaxed at your sides	In your pockets or touching other parts of your body
7	When asking for something, your hands are . . .	Palm down	Palm up	Crossed arms, or hands in pockets
8	When thinking . . .	Steeple finger/prayer hands	Thumb and pointing-finger grasp chin	Bite lips, or hands touch or rub face, cheek, mouth, bridge of nose, or hair
9	When walking . . .	Swing arms, elbows out taking up space, swagger	Hands are close to sides; arms move slightly	Hands in pockets
10	When listening to someone . . .	Look at the person you are talking to, head straight	Tilt head slightly, look at person you are talking to	Little eye contact, head turned away and ears face the speaker

11	How do you make eye contact?	Look at entire face, including forehead and mouth	Focus on triangle from eyebrows to tip of nose	Look down and not directly at the person
12	When you are upset, you wear a . . .	Disapproving frown/snarl	Blank face, no smile, tightened jaw	Pursed lips
13	When talking with someone less than a minute, your belly button faces . . .	Person you're talking to and hands are on your hips	Person you're talking to (and if hands are in pockets thumbs stick out)	Away from person you're speaking to (and if hands are in pockets thumbs are hidden)
14	When you're sitting with someone . . .	Directly across	Diagonally or right next to them	Unsure, never paid attention
15	How quickly do you nod your head?	Quickly	Slowly, moderately	Very slowly
16	Your sitting position at a boardroom table . . .	Taking up space, relaxed, lean back, elbows out	Hands relaxed and open, resting on the table	Hands folded on or under the table
17	When leaving a room with someone else, you . . .	Put your hand on her upper back and guide her out	Direct her toward the door and let her go first	Walk through the door first
18	When conducting a ten-minute small meeting around a table, do you . . .	Stay standing the whole time	Stand for the first few minutes, then sit	Sit down immediately, then begin talking
19	How is your posture when you are sitting?	Shoulders pulled back, sitting straight up	Comfortable, leaning slightly forward	Relaxed and leaning back
20	When ready to leave a meeting, you . . .	Touch the other person's upper arm or leg and announce it's time to go	Belly button turns toward the door, hands gripped on chair, ready to lift your body and excuse yourself	Sit and wait until the conversation is over and someone else ends the discussion

NOTE: To see actual pictures of all the gestures noted in this quiz, visit the online version at www.yousaymorethanyouthink.com.

BQ Answer Key

OVERCONFIDENT/ARROGANT

If your highest total number is in Column A, you may unconsciously be sending signals of arrogance. When you're nervous about what others think of you, you tend to overcompensate. It is this overcompensation that may make you look overconfident and it puts others off. You find it a challenge to acknowledge or come to terms with your own weaknesses, but you have no trouble pointing out others' (and you probably are irritated with me for saying that). Although a splash of the authoritative and dominating body language gestures in this column is powerful, when you use more than two at a time you can intimidate others and you can hinder the success of a project that relies on teamwork. However, if there is a sense of urgency to what you need done or an emergency, using any combination of these gestures will capture people's attention quickly.

Your Mantra: "It's only arrogance if you're wrong."
—Author Unknown

Your Success Killer: Impatience. (You might not admit it, but you know it's true.)

CONFIDENT

If your total highest number is in Column B, you're a natural leader. You have the perfect mixture of poise and confidence. You accept responsibility for your actions by taking ownership of your life, you evaluate yourself realistically, and you humbly know that you have the power to influence situations. You have the ability to command attention when necessary, but are flexible, empathetic, and build rapport with ease. You see life as a series of challenges and push yourself outside your comfort zone to get an edge on the next big thing. People are happy to see you because you're interesting and you're a great listener. Your open and engaging posture and gestures makes you easy to be around others, and they don't feel threatened or judged when they approach you.

Your Mantra: "Confidence comes not from always being right but from not fearing to be wrong."

—*Peter T. McIntyre*

Your Success Killer: When life throws you a curveball, it slightly chips away at your confidence level. (I'll let you in on a secret: you're still so extraordinary that no one else notices when your confidence slips.)

ANXIOUS

If your highest number of answers is in Column C, you may be giving others the impression that you lack confidence in yourself, your position, or your company. You may be hiding behind the self-given label of "shy." You often avoid situations where you fear you might be unsuccessful, humiliate yourself, or let yourself or others down. Oh, you might volunteer occasionally to be a member of the new focus group at the office, go on a date from the Internet (so you can say that you're "trying to break out of your shell"), or take on a new challenge when you have no choice. Regardless, you'll sabotage your success by either only doing it halfheartedly or complaining ("It's too much for me," "I'm confused," "I'm too busy with other projects," "There are no good men out there," etc.). You think people are constantly judging you and sometimes you feel like you're all alone.

Don't worry, you're not alone. Even famous actress Sally Field once said, "It took me a long time not to judge myself through someone else's eyes." (*Quick Tip:* people are not thinking of you half as much as they are thinking of themselves.)

Your Mantra: "When I turned two I was really anxious, be-cause I'd doubled my age in a year. I thought, if this keeps up, by the time I'm six I'll be ninety."

—*Stephen Wright*

Your Success Killer: Negative self-talk. (You tend to label yourself shy, stupid, ugly, fat, dippy, lazy, a procrastinator, a baby, etc.)

SELF-ASSURED/ALMOST ALWAYS CONFIDENT

If your answers are almost equally divided between Columns A, B, and C, you are on your way to being all that you can be. You just need to believe in yourself a bit more and understand that you are in control of your life. When you make a mistake, don't beat yourself up—instead, figure out what you can learn from that experience. And stop saying, "Not today, maybe next time" and start saying, "Why not? Let's do it!" Your body language is powerful when you're prepared and know your subject, but when you are challenged or not properly prepared, your body language leaks the silent message of self-doubt and nervousness.

Your Mantra: "Regardless of how you feel inside, always try to look like a winner. Even if you are behind, a sustained look of control and confidence can give you a mental edge that results in victory."

—*Arthur Ashe*

Your Success Killer: Giving up on yourself when the going gets tough. (And thanks to your closed body language, others notice.)

Once you have completed these five tasks, you are ready to begin the New Body Language program. Sleep well tonight—because tomorrow you're going to take on the world.

Day 1: Walk in Their Shoes

> You never really understand a person until you consider things from his point of view—until you climb into his skin and walk around in it.
> —*HARPER LEE (1926–),* To Kill a Mockingbird

In the summer of 2004, Special Agent Susan Bray, aka Sissy, was the lead ATF agent on a big firearms trafficking investigation of the Latin Kings street gang in Chicago. Although many Latin Kings had been arrested in a roundup, one member, Jody, had escaped prosecution because of lack of evidence. Jody's brother Jamie, however, was not so lucky—several days prior to the roundup he had been killed by members of his own gang. Given this dramatic betrayal, Sissy knew Jamie's murder trial would be an excellent opportunity to covertly gather insight and evidence for her investigation.

She attended every court date and noticed another young woman did as well: the mother of Jamie's child. The woman apparently held a grudge against Jody, with good reason. Jody had known about his brother's impending execution but did nothing to stop it. She wanted revenge and would do whatever she could to get it.

The young mother quickly became Sissy's informant. She gave Sissy information on the gunrunning operations and pretended to buy a gun from Jody while wearing a hidden recording device. The tapes revealed conversations about gun trafficking, but also his side job: refurbishing and reselling houses.

Once Jody sold a gun to the informant, Sissy had what she needed to

Name: Shilpa Patel
Age: 34
Occupation: Attorney

What was holding you back? I have always suffered from severe shyness. I assumed that if people were interested in me, they would approach me first; if I approached them, I would be bothering them. Anytime I had to speak, I would freeze up. I tried to copy other people's open, energetic, outgoing body language, but I looked even more ridiculous.

I'd gone to dating events with hundreds of men and not had a single date. For the Indian community, the age of twenty-five is past prime to get married, so as I neared thirty-four, my family was in a panic. I also kept myself in a dead-end, back-office law specialty so that I never had to go to classes or networking events. I've longed to do "real" legal work, to have the confidence to interview witnesses and prepare cases for trial. Despite this, I avoided giving my résumé to anyone.

How have you changed? Before I was alive but not living. I went through the motions, but things happened *to* me. I thought, *If only I had confidence like other people, I, too, could get what I wanted.* The day I started Janine's class, I took responsibility for my life. I learned to stop waiting for others to "carry" me along.

Today, I see everyone in a different light. I do not expect others to know what I am thinking, especially when they first meet me. I make a conscious effort to speak up at work and in social situations. Since the class I have had a few interviews and I'm not afraid to ask questions or play up my strengths, as I was before. I learned that being shy is selfish in a way, because you are expecting others to do the work that you should be doing.

I once heard the saying, "Everything will work out in the end, and if it has not worked out, it is not the end." Since the makeover I got two interviews with a government agency. My life has forever changed in the positive direction. I feel more happiness and contentment. I still have goals and I long to do more things, but I am at peace with myself and who I am.

arrest Jody. After reading him his rights, Sissy asked him if he wanted to talk. "No hablo ingles," he mumbled.

"That's okay," she smiled. "I pretty much have you dead to right on the firearms stuff. I'm more interested in the refurbishing. I know you're doing a couple of houses and your work is impeccable." She began asking questions about what steps to take, services and equipment to use, and so on.

"I do everything," Jody said proudly.

"That's good to know," Sissy replied genuinely. "Because I'm redoing my house and I might have some questions along the way."

Every time Sissy saw Jody after that, she would ask for his advice on remodeling her home. Like many others whom she had arrested, Jody began to think of Sissy as his friend. (Another criminal had once told her, "My lawyer said not to talk to you, but when we talk, I forget you're an ATF agent. I feel like I'm talking to a friend.") Instead of launching right into a discussion about guns or the Kings, things that might cause Jody to become distant and silent, Sissy and Jody first chatted about plumbing, insulation, and hardwood floors. Sissy would casually say, "I just painted the walls in my kitchen yellow and it brightens it right up," then segue immediately into, "I know that before your brother was killed he was taking the guns up from Mississippi, then you took over, so who will take over now that you're going to jail? I know that some of the other Latin King members are coming out soon. Will they start running the guns?"

To let Jody know that she knew more than he thought she did, Sissy would always bring up specific and personal information about Jody and the Kings. Jody would confirm Sissy's intelligence and her predictions with a cat-ate-the-canary grin, and when she was wrong he would flash a blank face that silently said, "Keep digging, my dear."

When his trial came, Jody decided to represent himself in court. In his opening statement, which he gave in shackled feet, he pronounced:

"I'd like to start by telling you that ATF special agent Susan Bray—I call her Sissy, and most of her friends do—she really is a good person. She's a *really* good person. She's really good at what she does. I like her a lot. But basically the informant got one over on Sissy. The informant lied to Sissy."

And as he was being escorted in cuffs from the courtroom before the jury deliberated, he turned his head to her and said, "It looks like you might be buying me a beer later to celebrate." Once Jody was out of the courtroom, the U.S. marshal gave Sissy a smirk. She smiled and said, "Please don't let him come back guilty. It's been a long time since I've had a date."

Shortly thereafter, the jury found Jody guilty. He was shocked. His eyebrows shot up and curved, his mouth opened in a quick expression of surprise. Then he hung his head and walked like a penguin out of the court with the shackles wrapped around his ankles.

Once Jody had been taken away, the same marshal grinned at Sissy. She shrugged and said, "Another one slipped through my fingers. Do you know how hard it is for a single girl in Chicago to get a date?"

Sissy's approach is not quite what you'd expect from a law enforcement agent, is it? Yet hers is a consistently reliable approach in any type of interaction: study your target, get to know him, and build trust and rapport on his terms—then move on to what *you* need.

The first step of this process, studying a person's natural behavior, is known as "baselining" or "norming," and it is the foundation of the New Body Language program. The reading and usage of body language effectively begins when you learn how to norm someone—and to norm yourself. Baselining and building rapport are such important skills that the ATF drills its new recruits on these skills more than any other. Once you have these two down, you can read and build rapport with anyone. Before you know it, you too can have hardened criminals eating out of the palm of your hand.

Accuracy: Find the Baseline— and the Probing Points

If you fail to take the time to study someone's normal body language signals, you will fall into two of the biggest traps of Old Body Language: mind reading and misinterpretation. In law enforcement, I've seen that oversight lead to wasted time focused on the wrong suspect and even, in tragic cases, to false confessions. Like this horrifying one: In 1998, in

Englewood, Illinois, two boys, seven and eight years old, were charged with murdering an eleven-year-old girl. Both boys weighed less than sixty pounds soaking wet. One of the boys had a speech impediment that made it difficult for him to communicate; as a result, his story changed slightly each time he told it to the four different interrogators who interviewed him. The police encouraged the innocent children to be "good boys" and to confess, and soon thereafter the boys were charged with murder.

Less than a month later the police were forced to drop the charges against the young boys. Why? Semen had been found at the crime scene that could not possibly be theirs—the boys' bodies had not yet begun to produce any.

Researchers cite this case as one of the most notorious forced false confessions in the history of Illinois. This case, and many other mishandled situations, could have been completely avoided with less than ten minutes spent baselining.

As you might imagine, the importance of baselining extends beyond catching bad guys and keeping innocent people safe. If you don't take a few minutes to establish someone's baseline body language, you are very likely to misinterpret his or her signals. In the business world, you may lose money when clients you misread walk away from a potential deal. Or you may lose employees or get passed over for promotions when you don't successfully "get a read" on your staff or your boss. And if you charge ahead without taking those critical few moments to study potential friends and lovers, you can end up with mincemeat made out of your feelings.

It takes just a few minutes to gauge a person's baseline and establish rapport, and you'll be ready to read and respond to any body language challenges that come your way.

Is it Personality—or Purposeful Evasion?

When you baseline individuals, you're looking for clues and examples of natural behavior, what they do when they're in default mode and not actively hiding anything. I find this one of the most fascinating parts of the New Body Language. In my head, I'm on Mutual of Omaha's *Wild Kingdom,* whispering to myself, "We're in the salesman's native habitat, studying his selling techniques. Notice how his eyes blink quite rapidly—maybe his contacts are drying out, or maybe he's nervous. He jiggles his foot quite a bit when he's talking. Is he hyperactive, or is that his itching to get away? We'll stay tuned to find out . . ."

I guarantee you, once you start norming people, it will become an addiction. You can learn so much from simply watching someone closely for a few minutes, without trying to judge his motives or read her mind. Just like anything in life, the more attention you pay to something, the richer and more layered the picture becomes. You'll start to see the wide diversity in humanity's norms. Take, for example, the vast differences between two iconic entertainers: Howard Stern and Woody Allen.

I don't think you could find two more completely different communication-based power players than shock-jock Stern and moviemaker Allen. In almost every photo taken of the edgy radio god, Stern's arms are relaxed and by his side. This is my favorite confidence pose

Say What?: *Left: Self-proclaimed "King of All Media" Howard Stern uses a confident and open stance. Right: Director and comedic actor Woody Allen hides his hands, making him appear anxious.*

of all. You've seen it in company newsletters or local newspaper clips of people receiving awards: the most powerful person in the picture will stand like Stern. The more nervous people or the subordinates in the photo will stand in the fig leaf position with hands in front of the below-the-belt area (what I call the "naughty bits"). Or they'll have crossed arms, or their hands will be buried deep in their pockets. Notice how Stern's hands aren't on his hips or behind his back, overstating his power. He's simply relaxed—whether you like Stern or not, that is confidence, baby! This open, totally secure pose would be Stern's baseline.

On the other hand, Allen has a completely different baseline. His norm consists of anxious facial expressions; folded hands, arms, and legs; lots of face touches; and slumped posture. In almost every photo taken of Allen while he's standing, his hands (including his thumbs) are hidden in his pockets. In most photos, he telegraphs anxiety, tension, and insecurity.

These two obviously represent dramatic extremes. Most people's body language is more subtle, located somewhere between these two ends of the spectrum. To get an accurate gauge each time, you need a disciplined approach, an objective process that takes emotion out of the situation and helps you evaluate each person based on the evidence given. And I ask you: What better tool to do that than a children's nursery rhyme?

Step 1: Head, Shoulders, Knees, and Toes

You're singing the song in your head right now, aren't you? This children's song is a great way to remember to look at every part of the body, not just the face, when you're norming someone. Just as kids touch each body part as they sing, "Head, Shoulders, Knees, and Toes" you'll learn to subtly do the same (with your *eyes*, of course).

You'll review people's bodies in these four areas and look for their default signals in each body zone. Check out the chart on the following pages for some of the most common signals and see how most signals have more than one meaning—which is why you have to see what's normal before you attempt to read anyone.

What's The Baseline?	A Change Might Mean . . .	Or Else Just . . .
HEAD		
Is the person's head tilted to the side, back slightly, or down?	Any later shift from the neutral position could mean you've piqued her interest.	That's just the natural tilt of her head.
Is the forehead wrinkled or smooth?	Based on the degree of wrinkles people hold in their foreheads when they are relaxed, additional wrinkles could mean anger or concentration.	Wrinkles could also mean aging—happens to all of us!
Where are eyebrows in their natural position?	Changes in the eyebrows could indicate interest/surprise (raised from neutral position) or anger/concentration (scrunched together).	Some people have unusually high eyebrows and look like they're constantly surprised.
How much eye contact does she give—40, 60, or 80 percent?	Increases or decreases could indicate anxiety or interest.	Shy people might feel more comfortable giving eye contact to people once they get to know them better.
Where do his eyes move to gather information?	Is he naturally "shifty-eyed" or will that indicate evasiveness later on?	Most right-handed people who are sensitive look down to their right when processing deep emotions, and down to their left when in self-talk mode. Sometimes lefties do the opposite.
Are her lips relaxed? What shape are they?	By knowing their natural size, you can later see signs of anger (when the upper lip disappears) or contemplation/disapproval (when she pouts or purses her lips).	She's using a lip filler or "Plumpers." These cosmetic options make lip baseline reading more challenging these days.
Is the bridge of his nose smooth?	If so, later a wrinkled nose could be an indicator of disgust (in an unconscious attempt to close up and keep something out that's offensive).	One of the women I coached on *Rachael Ray* scrunched her nose up when she laughed— very endearing!

SHOULDERS		
Is she slouching?	If a person starts with straight posture and then her upper body slouches forward, she may feel inferior or be losing interest.	Good posture is not a constant; some struggle to maintain it, even celebrities on TV. During a televised interview with Campbell Brown, the anchorwoman admitted that her mother constantly hounds her about her posture.
Is she touching her face, hair, clothes, or other parts of her body? Are her arms crossed?	When we're nervous or anxious we tend to use our hands to touch and subconsciously soothe ourselves. And most people, when they're comfortable, will relax their hands or use them with ease while making a point.	When I'm tired or cold, I'll cross my arms—who doesn't? It doesn't mean I'm anxious or close-minded.
Is his posture perfectly erect?	He could be sending the signal that he's uptight, apprehensive, or frightened.	John Wayne had extremely straight posture that people considered masculine and intelligent, but straight posture was simply his norm.
Are her shoulders parallel to you?	If so, a later change to a dramatic, angular distance between the two of you may reflect discord.	Some people feel more comfortable or "safer" when their shoulders are pointed away from others.
Where are his belly button and naughty bits (groin) pointing?	When his upper body leans toward another person, that could indicate interest; leaning away or pointing toward the door could indicate that he's formulating an exit strategy.	The lean may be due to pain or injury; an attendee at a recent seminar at Lockheed Martin told me that when the lower right side of her back begins to hurt, she'll lean to the right to lessen the pain.

Continued

KNEES		
How is he sitting—back into the chair with legs crossed over knees? Or leaning forward	When knees are engaged and legs are tense and appear ready to lift his body, this is a pretty good indicator that he's ready to leave.	When my dad sits too long, he stretches out his knees. It doesn't mean he's ready to leave or doesn't like what you're saying; he just has sore knees.
Is he sitting in the figure four position, with one ankle across his opposite knee?	This confident pose basically says, "Look what I have to offer." Because this position takes up more space, it is often perceived as extreme confidence.	These days, many people of either gender choose this position when they're comfortable. (It's a favorite sitting position of Rachael Ray and Ellen DeGeneres.)
TOES		
Is she sitting or standing up on her toes, as if she were defying gravity?	Cops often make this move when they ask you, "Do you know why I pulled you over?" It can indicate extreme confidence. When everyday people do it, they tend to be excited, as if they were floating on air.	My godmother Pat is barely five feet tall. When she's sitting, her feet don't touch the ground, so she'll often gain stability by connecting with the floor with just her toes.
Are her ankles crossed, wrapped around the leg of the chair?	Typically when people are close-minded or they're not planning on actively sharing or participating, they'll pull their legs in underneath their seat. And when they're self-restraining their emotions or thoughts, they'll wrap their legs around a chair.	People who suffer from social anxiety disorder or severe shyness can often be seen sitting with their legs pulled back under the chair— it's their norm.
Does he constantly move his body: bouncing his feet, crossing and uncrossing legs, making overly dramatic facial expressions?	Excessive movement could indicate nervousness.	Or ADD (attention-deficit disorder).

Are her ankles crossed?	Because crossed ankles take up less room than feet that are spread apart, this signal could indicate doubt in herself or what she's saying or self-doubt, a close-minded attitude, or that she wants to be someplace else.	Female students from the South will often tell me their mothers and grandmothers always raised them to sit with crossed ankles. They were told it's the way a lady sits. It's their norm.
Is his foot twisted with the sole pointed inward?	He may feel uncomfortable or uneasy.	My uncle Francie would turn his foot slightly inward because of a sore on the bottom of his foot that later turned out to be cancer. Many women in high heels make this move at the end of their day to ease the pain.

See how tricky "mind reading" would be? If you jumped to the first conclusion for any of these signals, you might miss the fact that they mean entirely different things to different people. That's why you have to study your target in a stress-free, low-key environment for two to ten minutes first, then wait for what I call a "Probing Point," the point at which the person departs from baseline behavior. Also known as a hot spot, this moment when a person shifts *from* his norm is when you *really* learn the most about his body language.

It's Game Time!

To improve the visual-perception skills that can help you quickly baseline others, challenge a friend or your child to a video game. According to *Scientific American* magazine, gaming a couple of hours a week not only improves hand-eye coordination, it also helps increase depth perception, boosts mental dexterity, increases attention span, and helps the players identify patterns quickly. Give in to your hidden desire to buy a Nintendo

DS or a Wii, or even head to your local video arcade for an hour or two. Scientists from Iowa State University found that laparoscopic surgeons who played video games performed their procedures faster and more accurately than those who didn't play. ○

Step 2: Mark the Probing Point

A Probing Point is the precise moment when a person moves from his norm to some other behavior. That change is the magic window into the New Body Language.

Think about Howard Stern again. Now that we know his norm is standing tall and strong with his arms at his sides, if he suddenly crossed his arms, put his hands in his front pockets, or stood in the fig leaf position (covering his private parts with his hands), we could recognize that Probing Point, and we could ask ourselves what's happening to cause it. Gestures that you don't see when you first norm someone carry special weight—they're signs of uncertainty, disagreement, deception, hidden attitudes, or unvoiced emotions. ˙

Here are some examples of how baseline behavior shifts at Probing Points.

Situation	Norm	Probing Point
Flirting	60% eye contact	>60% or <60% eye contact
Job Interview	Relaxed and open body language	He crosses arms and legs, creating a barrier.
Business Negotiation	Leaning back, while steepling	He leans forward and uses the honest and sincere open-palm gesture.
Buying a Car	Hands on hips with feet more than ten feet apart	His hands go into pockets (with his thumbs hidden) and his stance narrows.

Confronting Someone	Facing you, with his arms relaxed down by his side	His face remains turned toward you, but his belly button turns and faces the door.
Making a Request	Relaxed facial expression	Her nose does a quick wrinkle and when she says, "Not a problem, I'll do a great job for you," she makes a shoulder shrug.

7-SECOND FIX

Increase Your Perceived Value

The Problem: In the photo on the left, the man appears to be an outsider to the group of women. He seems to be making a move, but the women do not look interested. So why move? These women actually have very little to do with his pickup plan—his strategy is focused on the rest of the room.

The Fix: Move to the center spot (perhaps order a drink, then turn around and stay there). This fix is clever for a couple of reasons. First, the person in the middle always appears to be the leader. Second, now he appears to be with the women instead of an outsider hitting on them. With this little move, you'll increase your perceived value in the eyes of *all* other women in the bar! Sneaky, but smart.

You can see why an accurate baseline would be the linchpin to this entire process. If Howard Stern suddenly began tapping his feet or manically scratching his nose, that deviation from his norm could reveal that he's holding something back. But if Woody Allen made these same gestures, you might not even think twice.

Now, how can this information help you read body language accurately and apply it skillfully? The establishment of a baseline is the foundational skill for everything you'll learn in the rest of the program.

So what story does your body tell? Do you say more than you think?

Application: Understand Your Norm to Build Rapport

Imagine having your handshake, posture, stance, and smile analyzed by thousands of strangers on live national television. Unless you hope to be the next reality TV star, that's probably not in your career plan. But in July 2008, twentysomething Dana, a smokin' hot, articulate, successful Hooters "girl" was up for a promotion to become a regional training coordinator. Inspired by Dana's flawless work history and engaging personality, Kat Cole, vice president of training, was willing to put Dana's leadership ability and bravery to the test. When Dana was contacted by producers from CNBC's business show *The Big Idea!,* hosted by Donny Deutsch, about her potential promotion, she looked at this challenge as an opportunity to show her boss and the world how much pride, passion, and belief she had in herself and the company she worked for.

That day I was the resident *Big Idea!* expert who was tasked to help Dana perfect her interviewing skills. The producers set up a mock interview: I would interview Dana first on video and we would discuss what worked and what needed more attention.

Dana was warm, friendly, and the kind of person you want to hug when you first meet. Her genuine enthusiasm and desire to do her best were immediately obvious—but her initial energy was a bit much for an interview, especially for a major leadership position within the company. During the mock interview, we saw a drastic transformation in Dana—her baseline confidence took a hit and it showed in her body language: overly uptight straight posture; a tense, inauthentic, nonstop smile; jumpy legs crossing and uncrossing; and a couple of anxious hair touches. She even proclaimed a couple times, "I'm just so nervous right now."

Who could blame her? But we talked about how Dana's nervous norms were going to sabotage her success. We needed to fix that.

I asked Dana to recount a story about a time when she felt extremely confident and in control of a situation. As Dana shared with me a specific story about motivating the girls on the floor, her posture relaxed, she uncrossed her legs, she leaned slightly forward, was engaging, and used some confident hand gestures that she had not demonstrated to me earlier.

Once she was in this confident frame of mind, all I had to do was draw her attention to her body language at that moment. It was as if a lightbulb had gone off in her head. Dana got it. She knew exactly what to do in the interview. And when the cameras started rolling, and Dana walked into the interviewing room to greet her boss, Kat, she knocked it out of the park! An hour later, when the three of us joined Donny on set, Kat offered Dana the position of regional training coordinator.

Know Why You Should Know Your Own Norm

The people in my classes are always *amazed* by what they learn about their own norms. This step may well be the most enlightening aspect of the entire program for you.

Before you can learn how to adapt your body language to any situation, you have to know what you're working with. You'll enjoy three major benefits when you know your own norm:

1. You'll Break Your Mind-Reading Patterns. Judge not, lest ye be judged! The more you know about how your gestures, stance, and other nonverbal signals might be sending mixed messages to others, the better you'll be at breaking the old mind-reading habits when judging the body language norms of the people in your life.

2. You'll Adapt Your Body Language to Your Message. You have to know the raw material you're working with before you can master these moves. Getting your baseline is like finding coordinates on a map—

without them, you'll never be able to chart a course to where you *really* want to go.

Let's say you want to let the auto mechanic know you can't be swindled—but you shove your hands in your pockets when you're nervous, which shrinks your physical size and erodes your personal power. You could wear a coat without pockets, to discourage yourself from retreating to this counteractive signal, even if you get anxious. Or, say you want to encourage your kids to work together on a household project, but you used a palm-down gesture in the past, which gave them the feeling of being bullied or dominated. Boom! Family "teamwork" explodes into arguments, bickering, and a communication breakdown. Once you know your norm, you can clasp your hands together instead— or even stick them in your pockets!

3. You'll Change Your Brain. Your body language doesn't just affect other people—it affects the way you think and feel about yourself. In one study, forty-one Rochester University students were asked to cross their arms or leave them on their thighs while solving anagrams. People with their arms crossed not only performed better but also persisted eighty seconds longer than those with their arms on their thighs, who surrendered in less than sixty seconds. The researchers suspected that the act of crossing their arms triggered the students' unconscious ambition to succeed and increased perseverance.

Many studies have examined how deliberate changes in your physical movements—forcing yourself to stand up straighter—can help you experience more positive emotions and thoughts. When we repeatedly practice these positive body language signals, we train ourselves to feel more confident overall. Even the simple act of crossing your arms can have a profound effect on your ability to concentrate.

Although you'll never be able to control every microexpression that flashes across your face, you need to know how you appear to others in a normal setting. Your normal, habitual gestures give off signals that you do not want, like a lack of confidence, uneasiness, or distance, and you might not even have a clue. All of these signals interfere with your ability to develop rapport, the unconscious emotional connection that helps

> ## YOU SAY MORE IN YOUR FIRST THIRTY SECONDS . . .
>
> Those first thirty seconds may be all you have to make a good impression. A recent study looked at how job applicants were evaluated by trained interviewers versus untrained novices. The candidates were taped during twenty-minute interviews with seasoned staffing veterans, then separately, untrained observers were shown the first thirty seconds of each interview. Both groups were asked to evaluate each applicant based on two success factors: self-assurance and likability. The result? The first impressions from both groups were nearly identical.

you influence people with your body language. By learning your norm, you can prepare for those moments when you have to consciously suppress your own hot spots. Knowing your own norm provides a foundation for building rapport, the key to getting what you want.

Get Connected Through Rapport

Up to 90 percent of success in selling depends on your skills for establishing rapport with your prospect or customer. And whether you're in sales or not, we are all in the business of selling ourselves. From the hiring manager conducting a job interview, to the single mom buying her first house, to the middle-aged man on his first date since his divorce, if we want to be successful, we must learn to build rapport.

Rapport building requires more than simply mirroring someone's behavior or "pouring on" the charisma and charm. True rapport is about empathy. It's about understanding the other person so well that you can experience the world through that individual's eyes. It's the ability to listen with sincerity to others, understand their values, and connect seamlessly with their emotions, which ultimately builds respect, and even more important, trust.

I'll never forget the day I heard a presentation by the two detectives who got thirty-two-year-old chocolate factory worker and serial killer Jeffrey Dahmer to confess to murder. As we watched slide after slide of the most inconceivably evil, disgusting, horrific sights that the detectives witnessed at Dahmer's home, every agent in the room was struck dumb. Each of us sat there, shoulders slumped forward, noses wrinkled, and arms either crossed in front of us or we were wringing our hands. As repulsed as we were, we were transfixed by their story—how did these two detectives get Dahmer to confess to murder, and to crimes that the police had no leads on at the time?

These guys were pros. Despite being surrounded by the haunting remains of Dahmer's violated victims, the detectives were able to suppress their feelings of rage and disgust. Highly experienced interviewers, they knew the secret to getting the truth was to build trust, and the best way to do that would be to find something they had in common with Dahmer. But what could two educated and respected police detectives have in common with a sex offender and serial killer?

Religion. Dahmer's parents, and especially his grandmother whom he had lived with for some time, were very religious. So the detectives talked about God and forgiveness, and how God would want him to give closure to families of their lost loved ones. Then they listened, and listened, and listened while Jeffrey Dahmer confessed to one crime after another, after another, after another, until he confessed to all seventeen murders.

Rapport building is the foundation upon which all your interactions with others is built. It is the framework of all successful relationships, even within a horrific situation such as the Dahmer questioning. If those two detectives could establish rapport with a psychopath like Dahmer, you can establish rapport with anyone.

These top ten rapport-building guidelines are used by the world's elite communicators. You can use them, too!

1. Ensure a Strong Introduction. Within the first seven seconds of meeting someone, he has already made his first impressions of you. This "primacy effect" dictates whether or not the person will trust you. Before you walk into a room, imagine the person you're about to speak with is your best friend, someone you've known your whole life. This technique is one of the easiest to master and will give you a head start on positive and likable body language.

Introduce yourself and say your name clearly so people can remember it. One trick is to say, "Hello, my name is [pause for a beat] Janine [pause] Driver." Visualize your name on the marquee at the local theater. If you don't treat your own name with the respect and dignity it deserves, no one will. Say the person's name not just once, but several times throughout the conversation. My rule of thumb is to say a person's name at least once every ten to fifteen minutes of dialogue. It has been said that the sweetest sound on earth is the sound of our own name.

2. Mimic, **Cautiously.** If you've ever read a sales technique or persuasion book, you've probably been advised to mimic or "mirror" your clients. Seeing someone use the same gesture, or hearing the same tone of voice, activates brain circuits involved in our feelings of empathy. When we feel connected or "the same" as other people, our brains begin to trust them and feel for them.

As powerful as the mirroring technique is, you must apply it cautiously. You don't want your client to start feeling like you're a pesky kid brother who's just imitating him. My best advice would be to tread lightly. Mimic the other person, but wait a beat or two, and do a similar move, but not the exact move. Yes, people relate to and connect better with people who are like them, but one gesture copied too quickly and you're busted! The rapport bridge will be broken.

3. Treat Everyone with Respect. At times it can be a challenge to meet people with different political views, lifestyle choices, or levels of fitness and health, but we *all* have something in common. We are all human beings and if you want to build trust, you must treat the other person with respect. Get in the same frame of mind. Don't "talk down" to people. Get at their eye level or below their level, so you can give the impression that you are alike and equal. When you treat others the way they want to be treated, *not* the way you want to be treated, you'll have no problem establishing rapport with ease.

4. Take Your Time. One of the biggest mistakes people make when establishing rapport with others is that they hurry. For example, chiropractors often see their patients for a total of less than ten minutes.

MATCH YOUR AUDIENCE'S ENERGY LEVEL

Keynote speakers who make it their mission to "pump up" and energize early morning audiences are tragically deluded. People like people like themselves. Morning speakers—whether in a conference room or a convention hall—are more apt to end with a happy and satisfied crowd if their energy level starts out closely resembling the audience's.

But I will never forget one New York chiropractor who took just two minutes to establish rapport with me before doing my adjustment. I remember walking out of his office and realizing I'd been in there for about seven minutes, but I felt like I'd known him for years—we even hugged! I've nicknamed him the Hugging Chiropractor. He underscored a very important lesson for me: even if you only have two minutes to establish rapport, take the time to really connect with the person in front of you. Pay attention to what her body language is saying to you and what you are saying to her through eye contact, handshake, posture, angle of your body, the direction your feet are pointing, and gestures. These are critical moments. Take your time.

5. Get Them Talking. When we were young, my mother always told my sisters and me, "Your power is what you give to others." After using that advice successfully throughout my fifteen-year career with the federal government, I finally figured out that she was right. (Sshh, don't tell her I said that!)

The rule is easy; get the other person talking. Ask open-ended questions ("Tell me about your summer. What are you looking forward to in your next position? Why would you like a job with our company?"). Let the other person speak. The only way the detectives found out what they had in common with Jeffrey Dahmer was to allow him to share. If you do the same, you'll have more information to work with.

6. Be an Informant. Share something personal about yourself. Be genuine. Be open and candid and people will connect with you better. For instance, when my mentor J. J. meets new people, even the bad guys, he always jokes and says he has three kids, "one of each." After they share a chuckle, he explains he has three beautiful and powerful daughters, and he knows what it's like to be a dad, or to have unconditional love for someone, or to do anything to protect someone you care about. He uses that personal information to create a genuine bridge to the person in front of him. When you use too many "tricky" tools, such as mirroring, to influence others, you can appear inauthentic and maybe even manipulative.

Also, be completely up front and tell people what to expect during whatever process they are in, whether it be a job interview or an interrogation. You can radically decrease a person's anxiety just by telling her, "The interview will be no more than thirty minutes. I'll ask you a series of questions that I've been asking all the candidates, after which you can ask me any questions you might have."

7. Use Touch Carefully. Touch is a powerful tool, but must be approached with caution. Rather than making your touches dramatic or too serious, use subtle contact to appear casual and unpremeditated. Only touch someone while you're making a positive point, such as complimenting her or laughing at his joke. Try lingering touches that are soft and friendly rather than short jabs, such as holding his arm or wrist while looking at and complimenting his watch. Or in the boardroom, usher someone out the door with your hand planted on her upper back. Subtle touches send the message, "I like you. I connect with you. "

Again, be careful: don't touch too long or too often. Frequent touching can seem annoying, like poking someone over and over. And too much touch can make you seem less confident in the same way that constant smiling does. Tread lightly.

8. Nod Attentively. One study found that doctors who nodded at their patients were judged to be more empathetic and accessible, and developed better rapport, than those who didn't. The trick is to nod just enough, but not too much. Short single nods are most effective— they tell the person that you're listening intently. Double nods seem like you're trying to speed the person up. Triple nods (or worse, one very slow nod) may be confusing and may end the conversation.

9. Be Adaptable. "That's just how we do it here." "I've always done it that way." "Well, if they don't trust me, that's not my problem."

Ouch. It pains me to even write those rapport-killing statements. The key to establishing rapport and control is through adaptabiity. Adaptability requires a flexible approach during all new interactions. Most people get comfortable with a certain approach, a certain rapport-building method, and tend to stick with it. But adaptability is a fundamental quality of a great communicator. If you resist acquiring this one primary skill, you will hold yourself back from achieving all that you can.

Ask yourself, "Am I adaptable? Can I modify my actions when they're not working?" Really be honest with yourself. If not, start today by imagining yourself in someone else's shoes. Honing that one skill will take you very far in the New Body Language.

10. Keep Moving. Want to make it seem like you've known someone forever, even if you just met? Break your meeting up into several stages, each with its own location. Every time we travel somewhere with others, we see each location as a new experience, building our impressions of a long relationship. Don't stick to one place on a first date: go to one place for dinner, another for dessert, and a third for drinks. Several hours will seem like several days (in a good way).

Car dealers do this—they meet with you in the lot, where they discuss the vehicles and features they offer. Then they take you into the lobby, where you wait for a few moments before they take you on a test drive. By the time they talk prices in their office, you have already been in four different locations, making it seem as if you have been considering your purchase for a long time (and are therefore more confident in it).

Courting a client for your firm? Meet him out for lunch, then show him around your building, and finish your meeting in a conference room. Just be careful that you spend enough time at each place to reestablish rapport. If you don't do that, you might seem rushed, hurried, or easily bored. Think of a movie montage: show each "clip" long enough to know what's going on, but not so quickly that you lose the thread of the film.

Now, sit and soak this all up for a bit. Then, when you're ready, get started on Day 1's exercises.

Day 1: Learn How to Establish a Baseline and Build Rapport

Your 7-day program officially begins right now! And today's lesson will form the foundation for the days to come. I've included several different kinds of exercises each day—some that you can do while you're out and about, some that you can do while curled up in bed. Do a mix of each type each day. As you finish each exercise, take five minutes to answer this question in your Body Language Success Journal: "How can this exercise help me get what I want in life?"

You'll continue to use the techniques you learn today during the week ahead and, hopefully, for the rest of your life. As you know by now, a rock-solid awareness of baseline behavior—other people's as well as your own—is the foundation of the New Body Language. The following exercises will help you develop a more complete sense of your own normal body language behavior.

▶ *Take Notes.* For the first hour of today, your mission is to norm at least three completely different "types" of people. Look for at least one of each of the following types: shy, powerful/confident, and arrogant/aggressive. In your Body Language Success Journal, on three different pages, draw a stick person of each of the people you are norming. Now use the Head/Shoulders/Knees/Toes model to scan each. Write a one- or two-word observation next to the corresponding areas of the body (such as, "head back, nose slightly up, shoulders slumped forward, hip tilted to left side, hands on hips, feet two feet apart"). Allow yourself to write with plenty of detail, but limit yourself to two to ten minutes of observation for each person (the length of time of a standard norm). Once you've done this exercise on paper today, continue throughout the week *without* writing it down. Practice this exercise often enough and you'll start doing it automatically—which is the goal.

▶ *Craft Your Art of Observation.* Based on a law enforcement training program developed with New York's Frick Collection galleries and the NYPD, FBI, and National Guard, this training tool has sharpened the ability of thousands of special agents and officers, helping them to pay closer attention to detail when describing crime scenes, suspect detentions, and interviews. (The Body Language Power Team always tell me this is one of their favorite, and most instructive, exercises.)

If you are able, visit a local museum or gallery and observe one piece of art for thirty minutes. Notice all the details: Who or what is the primary focus of the artwork? Secondary focus? Why was this piece created: Was it the artist's personal interest? To earn money? To reflect society? To stimulate the brain, reveal truth, create beauty, protest injustice, immortalize an event or person? How did this aim influence the artist? By taking the time to articulate the elements of the piece on such a minute level, you sharpen your ability to notice details in other situations. Then ask yourself: How can I relate this piece of art to my life and what I want?

▶ *Find Out How Others See You.* Photocopy the BQ quiz from Chapter 1 and ask three people to evaluate you. See their answers as helpful, not judgmental. If their answers are different from yours, find out why. Ask them but *do not* attempt to change their minds. This makeover isn't about them; it's about you and how others are perceiving you.

▶ *Use That Mirror, Mirror on the Wall.* Stand in front of a full-length mirror; if you don't have one, find the largest/longest mirror you can.

Phase 1: Get Smaller

Step 1. Close your eyes.

Step 2. Recall a time that you were nervous, depressed, worried, or fearful. Think about the situation, how you felt, what you saw, what you heard, and what you did.

Step 3. Open your eyes. Observe your body language, facial expression, posture, and any other noticeable changes. Did you get smaller (hands in pockets, slumped shoulders, arms crossed, feet close together)?

Phase 2: Up on Your Toes—Defy Gravity

Step 1. Close your eyes again.

Step 2. Think of a time when you felt hopeful and excited. Once again, put yourself back in the place where it happened, reliving as much detail as possible.

Step 3. Open your eyes and note what your body language looks like here. Is your head up and are you smiling?

Phase 3: Get Bigger

Step 1. Get comfortable and close your eyes.

Step 2. Think about a time that you were confident and self-assured, when you knew you were going to win, when you were unstoppable. You did something even you didn't think you could do and you succeeded.

Step 3. Note your body language. Did you get bigger (head up high, shoulders back, hands on hips, wider stance)?

Next time you are in a situation where you are uneasy, change your body language so it matches what you saw in the mirror when you were excited or confident. These tiny physical changes can completely alter your perspective.

▶ *Become Your Own Reality TV Star:* Tonight, wherever you're going to be, bring the camcorder.

Step 1. Put it on a shelf or in a place that you'll forget it's there, and videotape yourself. You must tape yourself for a minimum of two hours (even if you're just watching TV).

Step 2. Before going to bed, watch one part of the video three times in the slowest fast-forward mode. Notice something different about your baseline each time you watch it. Do you sit on one of your legs? Do you wrinkle your forehead when you are thinking or bite your lip when you're bored? Do your feet move constantly? Do you play with your cuticles or wiggle your toes? And what about your posture?

Step 3. Write down your observations in your Body Language Success Journal.

▶ *Use the 5 in 15 Rule.* Appropriate touching can have an immediate, powerful effect. Touch is one of the most enjoyable activities in flirting and dating, and experiments have shown that even the most fleeting touch can have a dramatic influence on our relationships. Polite requests for help or directions, for example, produced much more positive results when accompanied by a light touch on the arm.

TUBE UP YOUR BASELINING SKILLS

Go to youtube.com and search for videos of these people:

- Johnny Carson, David Letterman, and Jay Leno
- Chris Rock, Robin Williams, and Ray Romano
- Frank Sinatra, Michael Jackson, and Miley Cyrus

Do each set as a unit, and watch a few short videos for each one. Notice their different norms by using the Head/Shoulders/Knees/Toes process: How do they cross their legs (and do they do it differently when with different people)? How wide are their stances? How do they use their hands when they talk? What's different about the cadence of their voices? Name at least three norms that are different among the people in each set ○

A good flirting rule of thumb is to touch a person five times within fifteen minutes. Here's a look at how you can use the "5 in 15 Rule" when you flirt with someone.

Step 1. FIRST TOUCH: Handshake

Step 2. SECOND TOUCH: Check out his watch or cuff links and keep holding his arm as you say something like, "I love your watch! It's sleek and stylish. My brother wants an elegant watch for his birthday. Where did you buy it?"

Step 3. THIRD TOUCH: When he says something charming or funny, lightly touch his upper arm or forearm and say, "You're so funny, [say his name]."

Step 4. FOURTH TOUCH: Do this "you're so funny" touch again after he makes his very next comment and say nothing—just smile.

Step 5. FIFTH TOUCH: Lightly grab his forearm or touch his hand and say, "Oh, I have to tell you the funniest thing . . ."

▶ *Practice Active Listening Head Moves.* As you talk with others today, use these various methods of nodding with head tilts.

1. Listen to someone, smile and tilt your head to the side, but *withhold all nodding.* Note what happens to the fluidity of the story. Does the speaker become uncomfortable?
2. Now tilt your head slightly to one side and nod your head while listening using single short nods. What happens?
3. Now try the head tilt with the double nod. Did the person speed up the conversation?
4. Finally, use a head tilt with the triple nod or the single, very slow nod. (*Note:* these nods will actually make you feel uncomfortable while doing them!)

The preceding experiments will help you determine when you should use each of the variety of nods with a date mate, the boss, your kids, or the judge. Try them out and see what works with each individual.

THREE

Day 2: Master the Belly Button Rule

I have learned to depend more on what people do than what they say in response to a direct question . . . and to look for patterns rather than content.
—EDWARD T. HALL (1914–), NONVERBAL COMMUNICATION PIONEER

My friend Jimmy Ebert was nicknamed "The Nose" because he could always sniff out much more than falsified paperwork and illegal explosives hidden in a closet. Now a senior investigator with the Alcohol and Tobacco Tax and Trade Bureau (TTB) within the U.S. Department of Treasury, Jimmy has a knack for reading people. He seems to get confessions in the time it takes some investigators to just establish rapport. Recently he was interviewing a suspect involved in a money-laundering scheme. Jimmy and his team of law enforcement officers arrived at the place of business early one morning, unannounced. During the interview, the suspect was sitting on a corner of a desk, facing Jimmy as he spoke with him.

As the questioning progressed, Jimmy noticed the suspect began to shift away from him. He turned his body to the right and started hunching his body over as he turned away. Jimmy said that had the suspect not twisted his body into what looked like an extremely uncomfortable position, he never would have asked, "Dude, why don't you take out what we both know is in your pocket? You're practically lying on your thigh hoping I don't notice the huge bulge you're trying to hide."

The suspect actually laughed and removed a wad of $4,600 in cash

Name: Clare Von Herbulis
Age: 31
Occupation: Project Manager in the furniture
industry

What was holding you back? I wanted to meet a
man who would love and care for me, someone fun,
genuine, and kindhearted. And handsome! But I was
almost never approached by men in person. About 99
percent of my dates came from online sites, but I was
rarely asked out on second dates. I was the "One Date Wonder." I wanted
to learn what messages I was sending through my body language—friends
and strangers often thought I was mad, guarded, upset, bored, scowling,
when I'd actually be in a perfectly happy mood.

How have you changed? My body language makeover was life transforming
on many levels. I became so much more self-aware. It's no wonder to me
now why my dates were not calling for a second date—my words and my
body were not conveying the same message! I was saying the words of an
open and confident woman, but my crossed arms, crossed legs, darting eyes,
and self-touches were screaming just the opposite. Now I'm more conscious
of where I'm facing so individuals know that they have my undivided
attention and focus in the conversation. The Belly Button Rule brings out a
different level of confidence and interest in people and holds their interest
longer. They feel more "pulled in to" or more engaged in what I'm saying
when my belly button is facing them.

Throughout my day, whether in the office, at the airport, at a happy
hour, or on TV, I am so much more aware of body language. I've realized
that the "dating principles" I needed to learn also have a great impact on
other aspects of my life, especially at work with clients and vendors. I now
send a louder message that I am prepared, focused, and knowledgeable.
People can see I mean business, hear my needs, and want to help me make
progress.

from his hip pocket. The newbie investigator who was with Jimmy in the room later said he felt like he was on a TV cop show—he was amazed Jimmy figured out what was in the suspect's pocket so quickly. "It's all in the body language," Jimmy told him. "The suspect subtly kept angling his belly button away from me, and that was a Probing Point. All I had to do was pay attention not only to his words, but to how he physically reacted."

Our belly buttons speak volumes about what we think and feel, and especially where we do and do not want to be. Let's look at the Belly Button Rule and how you can use it to gain valuable information in seconds.

Accuracy: See the Belly Button Rule in Action

Our first relationship with another human being is marked with a tiny little circled scar in the center of our body. From a businesswoman in Atlanta to a tribesman in New Guinea, everyone in the world has one. But this cute little lint holder has more power than you could have ever imagined.

The idea for the Belly Button Rule was initially discovered in a study by W. T. James in the 1930s. Through a series of tests that had respondents identifying almost 350 different meanings for various poses from a series of photographs, James was able to determine that the direction of the torso plays a key role in determining a person's level of interest. James separated belly button directionality into four key groups: approach (interest), withdrawal (disinterest), expansion (heightened interest and confidence), and contraction (nervousness and slightly reduced interest). About thirty years later, Dr. Albert Mehrabian further refined James's studies, noting that belly button direction was the most important aspect of reading a person's intention. Numerous studies have appeared since that time, confirming that the Belly Button Rule is one of the most accurate ways of gauging a person's interest and intent.

The direction our belly button faces reflects our attitude and reveals our emotional state. When we suddenly turn our navel toward a door or an exit or simply away from someone, we subconsciously send the signal that we want out of the conversation and perhaps even out of the

Using the Belly Button Rule in the boardroom can help reveal more information about the battle for power.

interaction. (I call it "navel intelligence.") As body language goes, the Belly Button Rule is one of the most accurate tools to read and influence others without them having to say a word. Many people don't know the BBR and don't have any idea how to camouflage this aspect of their body language. Once you learn to apply it, your accuracy at reading people will shoot up dramatically.

Belly Button Rule in the Boardroom

The BBR can be extremely useful in business situations. For instance, let's say you are sitting around a conference table, having an intense discussion about strategy. Suddenly you see one of your employees angling her navel in a new direction during a discussion about revenue numbers. That shift may indicate a hidden emotion, a difference in opinion, or a lack of interest—thus yielding you a perfect Probing Point.

The BBR can also help you gauge someone's loyalty or respect for your leadership. In the photo above, notice how the belly buttons are telling a

---

SAY WHAT? NAVEL INTELLIGENCE IS JOB NUMBER ONE

Warning: To avoid pulling out your hair every Monday morning, start the week off right and direct your belly button toward your boss and increase your odds at boosting rapport. According to researchers at Indiana University, rapport with the boss largely predicts risk for depression and other psychiatric problems in the workplace. A study published in the journal *Work and Stress* found that a worker's relationship with his boss is nearly equal in importance to his relationship with his spouse when it comes to overall well-being, no matter what the work sector. Even friendly coworkers or a rewarding occupation cannot compensate for a negative relationship with the boss.

---

very different story from what the upper bodies are saying. While some belly buttons face toward the leader of the boardroom meeting, others face away from him and toward the woman steepling at the other end of the table. Regardless of the direction of everyone's heads, this indicates that their interest (or loyalties) lie elsewhere. Many of the people around the table are facing the female manager seated across from him, so we may infer that that she is the real leader of this group. Note that her belly button is directly facing him, and her posture is leaned forward, suggesting confrontation. The meeting leader is leaning back, however, with his belly button facing upward, a sign of indifference and a lack of interest in his own meeting.

Belly Button in the Barroom

Belly button positioning is also very useful in social situations. You can save a lot of time and second-guessing if you can recognize a person's genuine interest, versus what he or she might want to show you. I'll never forget the night my friend Amanda begged me to go on a blind date with her. The catch? I was to hang out in the bar and spy on her date's body language. As you can imagine, I was more than delighted to help out. To make the evening even more fun, we decided if there was a problem I would text message her with the words "Code Red." That was an immediate alert for her to meet me in the bathroom.

There were many Code Reds that night—and they all had to do with the Belly Button Rule. In Amanda's case, she didn't pay attention to what his belly button was saying. He needed a little space, and his belly button was screaming that he was uncomfortable and wanted out of the conversation. My advice to Amanda was to redirect her navel to create some distance and give him his space. Once she truly got the Belly Button Rule, she no longer needed me as a hidden third wheel.

On the flip side, consider this photograph.

A woman speaks to one man but indicates her interest in the other with the Belly Button Rule.

Although the woman is facing the man on the right with her belly button, her face is pointing at his friend on the left of the photo. She is far more likely interested in the man on the right—but if he didn't know the BBR, he might be confused or even discouraged by her lack of "face time." By using these two opposing body language signals, this woman is cultivating an aura of mystery and keeping her options open. (See "Use the Belly Button Rule to Create Mystery," on page 74.)

On the other hand, if you are looking to approach someone new, check the position of his belly button to gauge his openness. When two people have parallel belly buttons, this suggests that they want to keep their conversation private. On the other hand, those angled away from each other—even if their heads are facing each other—are open to others joining them.

Belly Button Rule with Your Teen

This technique is especially useful with a group of people who tend to lie more than others: teenagers. What happened if you found a pack of cigarettes or condoms in your teenager's dresser? More than likely, when you confront her, she denies any knowledge or direct responsibility for them. ("They're not mine, Mom—I don't know where they came from.") When someone's belly button faces one direction but the eyes quickly glance at another—a drawer, closet, door, or any other location that might house a questionable object—take note. Nervous teens put their backs to what they want to protect, just like a mother lion protecting her cub. If she refuses to direct her belly button toward the drawer where you found the incriminating evidence, it's practically an admission of guilt. Also a familiar situation with teens: when confronting them about a potential lie, notice if their belly button suddenly points to an exit—that's a good indicator there's more to the story than they are telling you. Liars tend to point to the exit.

The Belly Button Rule, while an incredible lie detector and gauge of others' feelings, can also help *you* maximize *your* personal and professional relationships. Let's talk about several ways you can use your newfound navel intelligence to get your thoughts across in a more effective way.

Application: How Not to Go Belly Up

Are you aware when the people in your life need a little break from you, or from the topic at hand? Do you pay attention to their belly button

7-SECOND FIX

The Belly Button Rule

The Problem: Notice how the mother (left) has her belly button facing away from her daughter, and the daughter (right) reciprocates by angling her belly button in the opposite direction. Imagine a beam of light coming directly out of their navels; the two would never intersect—they're headed in two different directions.

The Fix: Align your belly button to your teen's, and you'll be on the path of open, respectful, and powerful communication.

barometer? When you see that belly button suddenly angling away from you, how do you change gears to win it back?

What about your own discomfort? Are you aware of the nonverbal signals you are sending to others with your navel direction? Is your belly button saying, "I want out of here," or beaconing to everyone, "Come talk to me"?

The Belly Button Rule helps you tune in to all the instinctive signals you may have felt before but never recognized. This tool is effective, easy to implement, and essentially the foundation upon which your first impression rests. You've been using the BBR all your life without even being aware of it—now it's time to consciously use it to your advantage. Check out a few situations in which, just by changing the position of your belly button, you can help change another person's mind.

Use the Belly Button Rule with New Contacts

Former President Bill Clinton is well known for making people feel comfortable, relaxed, and open with him, even if they have only known each other for a short time. How does he do it? It all has to do with the introduction. Whenever he meets someone new, even if it is one person in a long line of people, Clinton uses the Belly Button Rule. Check out the photo below.

President Clinton, a master of the Belly Button Rule, uses his navel to indicate his interest and to establish rapport. (Photo by Getty Images)

Clinton shakes hands with a local Norway politician, Svein Ludvigsen, with his belly button pointed directly at him. The former president almost always does this—he points his belly button parallel to whomever he's shaking hands with, gives the person a good handshake, shows a warm smile. And here's where his genius comes in: after he lets go of the individual's hand and moves to the next person, he keeps eye contact on the first person for an extra second, as if to say, "I hate to let you go." Even in a long receiving line, he'll persist in BBR-ing the first contact as his hand reaches for the next handshake.

Interestingly, his wife, Secretary of State Hillary Clinton, seems to

Secretary of State Hillary Clinton does not seem to have mastered the Belly Button Rule. (Photo by Getty Images)

do the opposite. In this photo Hillary shakes hands with people attending a rally on the West Lawn of the U.S. Capitol in Washington, D.C.

This is a trademark Hillary shake. In a long receiving line, she often uses a relaxed soft hand touch, her right hand extending to one person and her left to another. Notice how her belly button is not turned in the direction of either of the women waiting to meet her—she appears to be doing a drive-by, not even making eye contact.

Now, seeing both of these norms, and knowing what we know about how these people are perceived, can you think of any adjustments you want to make in your own body language? A warm handshake with a direct BBR connection can put you light-years ahead in establishing rapport. But a halfhearted handshake with your belly button turned away is essentially the same as giving someone the "cold shoulder"—which, when employed consciously, can also be quite useful.

Use the Belly Button Rule as a "Cold Shoulder"

Our instincts and common sense tell us that when we turn away and increase the physical distance between ourselves and another person, we give off negative, critical vibes. Often we can't help it—but once you become aware of this effect, you can use it to your own advantage. When you face away from someone, and give him the "cold shoulder," you also provide yourself an exit. This might also increase your desire to leave the situation, which could increase your courage to do just that—often helpful when you need to disengage from a pestering salesperson or a lecherous barfly. In certain situations, you can even use it with your family—to ferret out the truth.

Use the Belly Button Rule as a Truth Magnet

The belly button doesn't just help you detect lies—it can help you draw truth and cooperation out of people too. When you're speaking with your teen, for example, you can show approval when she agrees with you or is truthful by facing your belly button toward her. But when she lies or holds something back, turn away. This strategic use of the BBR to communicate disapproval of lies and approval of truth can subconsciously spur her to *want* to please you with more honesty and cooperation. Clever, huh? That's how effective the BBR can be.

Use the Belly Button Rule to Create Mystery

Here's another technique that uses the BBR to your advantage. According to Rutgers University professor and world-renowned anthropologist Dr. Helen Fisher, people are excited by others who are mysterious, because mystery triggers dopamine, a potent stimulant in the brain that gives us a natural high. Knowing the BBR is also powerful, you can use both to make yourself nearly irresistible to others.

When you meet someone you're interested in, you know to check to see if your belly buttons align. If they do, you can be certain the other person is interested too. Now let's say you want to draw him in further. After a while, move your belly button slightly away from your new friend to a more open position, but continue to smile and flirt, and even get some touches in. The contrasting signals will create a bit of mystery and make your new friend eager to reestablish direct belly button connection.

When at work, at home, out to lunch, or pretty much anywhere, start keeping an eye on people's belly buttons (and not just those of people who are talking to you). After careful observation of others, try your own belly button tests. When you face someone with parallel belly buttons, do you feel more connected or confrontational? Are you more relaxed when you open your belly button to include others in your conversation? What belly button position makes you feel more confident? Is there one that makes you feel less confident?

Change your belly button position while talking with others and see how it changes the conversation. Do they become more interested? Less? Does the mood change? Do you still have the same rapport with the other person? Note what you did and the results, and keep building on that knowledge.

Day 2: Master the Belly Button Rule

Remember that the BBR is one of your most powerful body language tools; it will help you improve quickly and cut your apprenticeship to a fraction of the time. Use the BBR and you'll tune in immediately to people's unspoken thoughts and be more focused in your own conversations. Pick at least two of the following exercises to complete today. As you begin to see the BBR at work in your daily life, you'll start to do this automatically.

▶ *Baseline Belly Buttons.* Observe three people (they can be the people you normed yesterday). Where do they face their belly button when interacting with others? Without them saying a word, what message is the direction of their belly button conveying to you? At night, look through your photo albums. Where are your friends', former friends', family's, and ex-mates' navels facing in the shots? Log your analysis in your Body Language Success Journal.

▶ *Read My Hips!* Sign up for a local belly dancing class and begin to build a relationship with all three sets of your stomach muscles: the diaphragm, which is between the navel and the rib cage; the pelvic muscles, which are below the navel; and the obliques which run vertically on each side from the pelvis to just below the breast. If you'd like to learn to belly dance in the comfort of your own home, just visit iTunes and download Shakira's "Hips Don't Lie" (if you don't already have it) and get ready to move those hips and roll that belly of yours! There are instructions all over the Internet on how to belly dance.

▶ *Reverse Your Belly Button Polarity.* Now that you know how powerfully our belly buttons want to attract each other, see what impact you can have when you don't obey the BBR. Walk around for part of the day facing your belly button *away* from people. Think like a magnet with two negative charges—actively repel others' belly buttons. What happens?

▶ *Do Some Extreme Belly Button Conditioning.* For you extreme adventurists out there willing to take a day off to test the BBR, go tandem skydiving! I've done it and I can tell you there is no greater test of the importance of our midsection, the core of our body, than skydiving. When you actually step out of that plane and feel yourself falling with the wind, you will forever understand the importance of not only how your belly button direction always faces your target, but how every slight move you make with any part of your body could put you in a compromising situation.

If you're not ready to "make the leap" just yet, practice in a skydiving tank before you set out to do the real thing. Many skydiving companies train students in skydiving tanks that provide you with the same sensation as being in the air.

FOUR

Day 3: Work Your Naughty Bits and Other Lower Extremities

Better to live one year as a tiger, than a hundred as a sheep.
—MADONNA (1958-), RECORDING ARTIST

felt like a prisoner within the walls of the FBI. It was the winter of 1998, and I had volunteered for an eight-month detail as an ATF/ FBI liaison, helping examiners in the National Instant Criminal Background Check System (NICS) understand firearms laws and regulations. Despite working for a federal agency and having a top-secret clearance, every day I was escorted from the demoralizing cubicle farm where they'd buried me to the photocopier, fax machine, cafeteria, and even to the bathroom—everywhere.

I missed the freedom and respect I had taken for granted while working for ATF in New York City's World Trade Center, where I had the ear of the director of industry operations and the special agent in charge. Many of my peers in the FBI treated me like an equal, but my superiors made it clear that I was an outsider. For most of the time at this new post, I thought I was being singled out for the cold shoulder treatment—that is, until one day right before my "sentence" was up. That's the day I saw the effect of this atmosphere on all the NICS examiners.

That afternoon, a few weeks before I was to return to my regular assignment, many of the FBI colleagues I'd been working with were called into a giant auditorium for an urgent, unexpected meeting. As everyone

Name: Michael Smith
Age: 45
Occupation: Certified Public Accountant

What was holding you back? I have just about everything I could hope for—I'm an all-American guy, college educated, white-collar professional with three kids, a dog, a gorgeous wife, and a house in the suburbs. But since hitting midlife, I had been asking myself, "Isn't there something more?" What about that last 5–10 percent of the American dream? What is most important, what is my purpose? I want to drink it all in and live life with no regrets.

If I were to pursue any self-employment or a high-salary position, first impressions and charisma will be critical to succeed. The same holds true for personal relationships. If I can project and interpret body language signals better, it can only help me to have better relationships.

How have you changed? Before I learned the Naughty Bits Rule, I was very comfortable with my hands folded in front of me in a fig leaf. I had no idea I was sending signals that I was unapproachable, or worse—that I had something to hide. Now when I catch myself trying to put my hands in my pockets or the old fig leaf, I'll switch to a hook position (if I'm in a casual setting) or I'll drop my hands to my side (if I'm in a more professional, formal environment). I think the technique has made me appear warmer because people are more likely to approach me and strike up a conversation. It's been very useful before meetings, during that time when everyone is standing around waiting for the meeting to begin, or afterward, when people are transitioning to lighter, more social pleasantries.

Before my body language makeover, life was dull and boring; I was trudging through the days and nights not really living. My mother's voice would play like a broken record in my head, "Don't talk to strangers." Not anymore! Now I can walk confidently into a room and, with the insights and tricks for reading people that I learned from Janine, I no longer feel any anxiety meeting or talking with strangers.

Overall, the 7-Day Body Language Makeover was like getting plastic surgery for my mind and body without the cost or pain. Since my transformation the world has become my playground, and the people in it are my new best friends. Life is fun, exhilarating, yet authentic.

got settled, the manager facilitating the assembly stood at the front of the room, like a statue. Once he began to speak, he was direct and to the point. No small talk. No smile. He just dropped life-changing news on them with the empathy of a rock.

"NICS schedules are changing immediately and these changes will impact many of you," he said. Some people would now be working weekends, others four ten-hour days, some the more traditional five-day week, and others would start their day late in the afternoon, and work into the early morning hours of the next day.

Nervous chatter rumbled through the room and hands shot up. The first guy yelled out, "Based on my current schedule, I registered for grad school. I've already paid the tuition. And I'm a couple months into my classes."

Another person shouted, "I'm a single mother and I can't work the late-night shift."

"Me, too," said another woman sitting on the edge of her seat, in the row in front of me—although she said it under her breath.

The FBI facilitator responded with all the warmth and empathy of a drill sergeant. "If the new schedule doesn't work for you, put in your resignation now," he growled. "Because for every one of you sitting here, there are a hundred other people who would love to fill your seats, and your new schedule!"

Ouch.

I watched as the one hundred–plus people who filled the room shook their heads in nervous disbelief. Clearly, many people were wondering, "What's my new schedule? If it doesn't fit my life, what am I going to do?" Just as you see the Wave work its way through a packed football stadium, group by group, row by row, people began to wring their hands in their laps and cross their ankles or their legs.

Watching this change unfold, my heart broke for these people. Theirs was the textbook display of what happens to our body language when we feel vulnerable and stripped of our value and personal power: we turn in on ourselves and close up, so as to subconsciously protect our most important body parts. Among them, of course, are our reproductive organs—or what I call our "naughty bits."

Accuracy: Watch Who's Flashing the Naughty Bits

What we do with our "naughty bits"—whether we direct them forward confidently or cower and hide them behind a hand, a crossed leg, or a crouched torso—is every bit as telling as what we do with our belly buttons. Much like your belly button, your naughty bits and lower extremities are great indicators of your interest in, or aversion to, certain people and situations. But while you only have one belly button, your naughty bits/lower body options have an array of parts—hips, groin, legs, knees, feet—that can communicate your message.

The naughty bits and lower extremities are certainly versatile body language tools, but their signals still break down into two basic groups: closed and open. When we cover our naughty bits, we appear threatened. When we expose them, our bodies appear bigger, more confident, less fearful. I'm sure you've noticed that this theme repeats itself constantly in body language, both among humans and in the entire animal kingdom: we make ourselves bigger when we're confident, and smaller when we want to disappear.

Hiding the Naughty Bits

One of my dear friends and mentors, Neal Earl, senior investigator at the ATF, uses the naughty bits to gauge liars every day. One September, Neal accompanied a local fire marshal along to a blaster's storehouse in Connecticut, to check out his storage facilities. (A blaster is a professional who uses explosives to demolish structures or displace earth.) Neal had traced a paper trail and discovered that although the small blaster had storage space for a maximum of five hundred pounds of explosives, within a three-and-a-half week period he had purchased explosives exceeding twelve thousand pounds.

At first, when the two officials arrived at the door, the blaster's body language was relaxed, his arms were down by his sides and his legs were approximately a foot and a half apart from each other as he stood. He clearly didn't think he had anything to worry about. But when he heard that one of the men was an investigator from ATF, he glanced over at Neal and immediately his arms moved into the closed-off fig leaf position. Holding the wrist of his left hand with his right hand, he covered his groin, and his stance shrunk by at least five inches.

Recognizing that his presence made this guy incredibly uncomfortable, Neal didn't say a word—but he spoke volumes with his body language. His posture was straight, his feet were three feet apart, his chin was slightly tilted back, and he astutely kept a constant eye on the blaster. Neal noticed the blaster look at him, then quickly glance over at his trucks, then look back again at Neal. "Okay, I might have a little more stuff over there in my truck," admitted the blaster. All three men walked over to the truck, where they uncovered nine hundred pounds of explosives, illegally stored in the truck overnight.

Neal's patience and strong presence wore this guy down, and each time Neal asked if he had any more, the suspect would first cover his groin, then relent and reveal a few more hundred pounds of explosives. Neal said it was like a scene out of the TV show *24*—but instead of brutally interrogating the guy, Neal just patiently studied his suspect's body language to learn the truth.

Once you start to notice how people obscure their naughty bits and lower extremities, you'll be amazed just how often people think they're being sly when their bodies are really screaming, "I'm afraid!" One of the most common signals that hide the naughty bits is the pose this suspect used, the fig leaf.

The Fig Leaf

You can't get a more direct naughty-bit cover than the fig leaf. In the classic fig leaf pose, the person will clasp his or her hands (and sometimes by the wrist), and place it directly in front of the crotch or lower belly. You see this pose all the time in staged photo ops, and at funerals and other formal, somber situations.

In any situation that's less formal, a fig leaf might indicate serious discomfort and anxiety. People use this pose almost instinctively, perhaps as a default pose that they consider respectful and businesslike. But

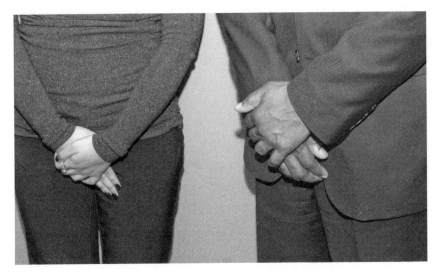

A fig leaf position usually indicates a sense of unease and anxiety.

many people read this move to mean fear, and they believe it telegraphs weakness.

Hands Shoved into Pockets

As part of their grooming standards, Marines cannot put their hands in their pockets while in uniform unless they are getting something out or putting something in their pockets. In contrast, this Woody Allen trademark stance is a popular one for shy or less confident people. These folks may think they're hiding their nervousness by shoving their hands in their pockets. They may think they're seen as more casual or confident because they don't feel compelled to do something overt or "stiff" with their hands. But honestly, any time a person hides a body part—especially something as important as his hands—people see it as a message of nervousness. (*P.S.:* we can tell when your hands are balled up in fists in your pocket—you're not kidding anybody.)

This move is also considered a self-touch gesture, or what other experts call manipulators, pacifiers, or adapters. It's an often unnoticed movement that we make where one part of our body (in this case the hands) touches another part of our body (upper thighs), usually to soothe ourselves during situations of high mental stress.

Crossed Ankles

Whenever I see someone doing this pose, I think, *Geez, go to the restroom already.* This pose makes a person, most often female, look like a little kid who is either bored out of her mind or terrified of getting in trouble. This pose makes you appear small, closed off, and as if you literally do not have both feet on the ground. In the business world, this move is often perceived as the physical embodiment of apology: "Really, I don't want to bother you—let me just say my piece and be gone."

When you've normed your employee, your customer, or preteen daughter and she always has both feet on the ground, pay special attention when she suddenly crosses her ankles if talk turns to meeting the

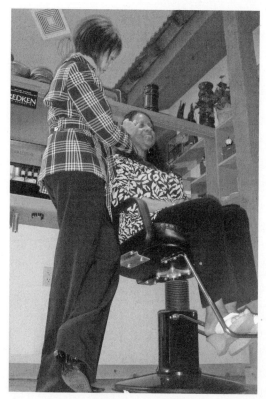

Crossing your ankles tends to weaken your appearance.

deadline, the increase in pricing, or the birds and the bees. Yes, she is getting physically smaller and closing down, but maybe it's because she's wearing new boots and her toes just started to hurt. Before you make the biggest mistake of body language and become a mind reader, simply take a break. Ask her if she has a minute to join you for a walk, either around the block or to the cafeteria, and continue to talk shop while you are both in motion. (When you move your body, you can move your mind and let off any built-up nervous energy.) Once back in the office, see if she resumes the same crossed legs and ankle pose—highly unlikely, unless that's her constant baseline!

Crossed Ankles Entwined Around Chair

Do you remember the last time you had one of those weeks when everything came crashing down on you all at once? You may have found yourself an unconscious solution—perhaps you wrap one or both of your feet around the leg of your chair. This common stress-relieving move is used in poker when someone is dealt a terrible set of cards and they want to drop the F-bomb, but they don't want to let people know they're in trouble. But it also shows up in boardrooms, classrooms, restaurants, and in job interviews.

Many people think this pose is simply a variation of the crossed ankles that many women consider the height of politeness. But when a person incorporates a chair into the ankle twisting, it's the same as chewing on a pen cap or rolling up the side of a paper in a meeting—if you need a prop, your nerves are headed for the roof. Wrapping your ankles around a chair either screams, "I'm so frustrated that I might break the leg of this chair," or "I'm insecure and nervous and want to get the hell out of here!" Either way, people are going to look at you and say to themselves, "Now, that's not a confident person."

The next time you notice yourself doing this, think instead, "Let Go and Say No!" The one positive use of this pose is when you feel like you are about to unleash a fury of angry, mean-spirited words on someone—then take a seat and wrap one or both legs around the leg of a chair, think of three things you are grateful for, and regroup.

The Undercover Bits

This smart, but gutless move is accomplished by either leaning forward on a table with your upper arms and pushing the bits backward with the chair, or by covering the bits with a jacket, or a notebook, or even something as unassuming as folded hands in the lap. This clever bit barrier often goes unnoticed by the untrained eye, but it still lacks power and authority. However, if you're extremely nervous, I'd much rather see a jacket across your lap than bouncing feet, crossed ankles, or intertwined ankles around the leg of a chair. But the trick is to give yourself a time limit on having the bits on lockdown. My rule of thumb is you have ninety seconds before you have to blow your cover, relax, and open up your bits.

Figure Four Bit Display

Admittedly, the figure four position, when the ankle of one leg rests on the knee of the other leg, does highlight the naughty bits—but it also gives an impression of being closed off, which is why I've included it here.

The figure four display could indicate nervousness, lack of flexibility, rudeness, or power—it all depends on the situation and the person's norm.

Certain additional factors influence how this signal can be interpreted. The direction your toes point can indicate attention or interest toward a particular subject. Bouncing or moving one's legs while seated can show nervousness. But the figure four is the most controversial bit display. To give you an idea of all the hidden messages this leg cross represents, here's how some of my students described it:

Argumentative
Arrogant
Closed
Confident
Defensive
Dominant
Least professional of all stances
Offensive
Powerful
Rude
Stubborn
Young and hip

If you observe someone displaying a figure four, you now know that depending on who observes this naughty bit signal, the perceived meaning could go a few ways—so it's best not to jump to conclusions. To be safe, I always recommend that, especially when the outcome of your interaction depends on a stellar first impression, neither men nor women use the figure four. Instead, if you're a man, simply rest both of your feet on the ground, spread them about three or four feet apart, flash your bits, and send a message of power. (Ladies, be very conservative; there's never a time when it's appropriate to flash your bits to get what you want, so focus more on using your power hand gestures to earn respect and professional admiration. We'll discuss those more in Chapter 6.)

Regardless of leg position, don't forget to remain aware of the person's norms. If a person starts a conversation with his or her feet parallel to each other on the ground, and then some time in the middle of the discussion, suddenly shifts into a figure four, fig leaf, or other naughty-bit-obscuring pose, that shift in leg position is your strong indicator that there is more to the story.

If you tend to hide your naughty bits, take heed: using these positions consistently can and will undermine your message of confidence. People may begin to think these poses reflect your regular internal state and paint a mental picture of you as weak. There are very few reasons to use these positions consciously—using them will likely make people think that you are a pushover.

Now, showing off the naughty bits—that's something else entirely. Step back!

Showing Off the Naughty Bits

Your naughty bits are like an Elton John or Cher costume—they capture a lot of attention even from the cheap seats. Positioning the naughty bits in a way that draws attention to them shows confidence and power, and says, "Look at what *I* have to offer!" Once you become aware of how the naughty bits can be worked, you'll see the signals all over the place: seated, as in the controversial figure four position or with crossed legs; standing with feet hip width apart (more on that below); or with hands or thumbs pointing at the area.

Now, based on how against I am to naughty-bit-hiding poses, you might think that confident, naughty-bit-revealing poses are the way to go here, right? Well, yes and no. If you meet a guy who's constantly thrusting out his pelvis like a Chippendale dancer, you might be more inclined to get a restraining order than his number. Working the naughty bits is all about subtle strength.

Crotch Displays

When men are confident, they'll flash their bits in what I call crotch displays. Some of these displays signal power and confidence (and are favored by people who are often unstoppable!). Others send the message of close-mindedness and argumentativeness.

The last time you grabbed a drink at your local watering hole, you may have noticed a man with his left leg on one side of the woman and his right leg on the other side. This pose is no mystery—he has clearly marked his territory. But if you're not sure about the message his naughty bits are sending, take a look at his feet. Feet always point in the direction of our interest, so combined with the Belly Button Rule and the naughty bits, you have a very reliable gauge of his interest before you even open your mouth. But if you can only catch one signal, one of the easiest ways to tell how a man feels about a situation is to examine his naughty bits. (I never dreamt I'd write that sentence in a book!)

One Leg Up Bit Display

When men and women put one of their legs slightly higher than the other, and they face their naughty bits outward, it makes them stand out. That one pose shows we've taken ownership and control of whatever our foot rests upon, whether it be a barstool, the bumper of a car, a step someone else is sitting on, and so on. Perceived "ownership" is the key building block when it comes to pushing people around, getting the upper hand during a negotiation, or dominating during a heated debate.

On the other hand, a raised outside knee with the naughty bits angled away from people and more toward a wall is usually an indicator of a desire for privacy or a lack of interest in those on the other side of the tensed leg.

Pocket Thumb Displays

Newborn babies either suck their thumbs or tuck their thumbs inside their fists because they are trying to protect and comfort themselves. Thumbs are clear indicators of your self-confidence level. What message do you send to others when your hands are in your pockets?

Many celebrities and world leaders favor thumb displays that signal more than confidence, authority, and power—and instead telegraph a clear message of superiority. John F. Kennedy worked his thumbs all the time. These days, Patrick Dempsey, Tim McGraw, Ryan Seacrest,

Work those power thumbs.

John Travolta, Brad Pitt, and Jennifer Aniston all do it. Keep an eye out for those celebrities whose hands are in their pockets, but who always stick out their thumbs—those displays are powerful signals of independence.

Instead of letting your thumbs rest on the outside of your pockets, you can put your thumbs in your pockets with the rest of your hand on the outside. This cowboy maneuver is called "Hooking." More on that in a minute.

Hooking

Hooking, hanging your thumbs on your belt, pants, or pockets, is not for the faint of heart. When the hooking is done by using one of the two front pockets it *really* highlights the "bits." It screams, "Have you checked out my bits today?" Notice photo A (on page 90)—how sexy and powerful is one-handed hooking? Very.

 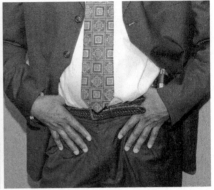

A   B

Also notice in photo A how the man's left leg is slightly higher than his left—this combination pose is a neat power move. Don't forget—when a person elevates one of his feet on to a woman's barstool, the bumper of a car, or the step a woman is sitting on, he's showing ownership of it (or her) to some degree. You might be open to that, of course—if you sense this combination move and are not interested, I recommend that you make your feelings understood soon after this display. If you don't want to be "owned," it's a really good moment to turn your naughty bits or belly button away to defuse the situation.

Hooking is *very* easy to overdo. Take a look at photo B. Cheesy overkill. Bad hooker. Down, boy. Two hooking hands can send the message of aggressive overconfidence and can repel people who don't want to be dominated (i.e., most of us). If you've normed someone and see him break out this signal, tread lightly. You're likely in the midst of an extremely confident person, perhaps even a bit cocky and arrogant.

By the way, ladies, I want you to know: hooking is not just for the boys. (Now get your mind out of the gutter!) If you're tired of looking blah, you don't need to run out for a new outfit. Simply throw on a pair of jeans and hook one of your hands in any of your four pockets (preferably one of the front two—that way it's noticeable). When a woman hooks her hand, she sends a message of spunk, supreme self-reliance, and sex appeal! Meow.

7-SECOND FIX

Workin' the Naughty Bits and Other Lower Extremities

The Problem: If you take a piece of paper and cover up this woman's lower body, you can see her face looks somewhat the same in both photographs. But remove the paper and you can see how much more confident she looks when she goes from the fig leaf position to working her naughty bits.

The Fix: If you notice yourself standing in the fig leaf, put your hands behind your back. It's really that simple; you'll send the message that you are confident and you have all the answers.

Application: Don't Hide—Unless You Must

"Be prepared. Make two lists, one of key dates and information and the other a list of your qualifications. Sit up straight. Speak loudly and clearly. Make eye contact. Answer each question truthfully to the best of your ability. State only the facts; the judge and jury will decide whether your testimony is credible and persuasive. And be wary of 'trick questions.'"

What? Be wary of trick questions? How will I recognize "trick questions"?

Moments before I was about to testify in federal court as an expert witness for the U.S. government, these statements, along with the box of tissues sitting there in front of me in the witness box, had me thinking: *Someone's going to make me cry today.* In the long list of well-intended motivational tips above, which I got from other investigators and special agents in my office who had already testified in court, the only thing that stood out in my mind was "trick questions."

I began to get nervous. Would I somehow screw up the case? Would I be tricked into revealing my weaknesses as an investigator, or as a human being? Would I let down the bureau and this country by putting a firearms trafficker back on our streets? I had to get it together. *Breathe, Janine,* I kept repeating over and over in my head.

Then my testimony began. I had to be asked to slow down my typical Boston-fast-paced speech because my testimony was being transcribed and the court reporter couldn't keep up. The U.S. attorney smiled at me and didn't seem to mind because the judge had me repeat my statements again, which meant that the jury heard them a second time. But I was nervous anyway. *Breathe, Janine.*

While my shoulders were pulled back, and I was maintaining great eye contact, my feet were bouncing a mile a minute and my hands were squeezed together tightly, buried in my lap, as my left thumb anxiously rubbed the top of my right hand. And in between each of the defense attorney's questions, my mind would race with impending thoughts of danger. What if the firearms trafficker's friends, who would inevitably be in court, followed me home that day? What if they found out where my parents and sisters lived? Was my family or I at any kind of risk?

Despite my nearly crippling anxiety, the defendant was found guilty in that case, and even the U.S. attorney commented on the validity of my testimony. My saving grace had been the three faded wooden panel walls that surrounded the witness box. Without that shield, the entire courtroom would've seen the full weight of my anxiety just by looking at my naughty bits and lower extremities.

Only Hide Your Bits When Absolutely Necessary

You might be scratching your head right now, thinking, "Um, is she recommending I hide behind a wall to obscure my body language? Is hiding behind a wall *really* learning to master my body language?"

My answer: Yes, absolutely. It's using another tool at your disposal, and it's all part of knowing your own norm. I knew I would be nearly incapacitated by my anxiety—but the show had to go on. So instead of crumbling (or crying!), I used what I could in the environment. I saw that the box would cover the lower two-thirds of my body, and in order to have a release valve for my nervous energy, I consciously pushed my nervous energy down below my waist. Not one member of the jury could see my legs bouncing around within those three walls, but it created a safety net for my jumpy nerves and allowed my upper body and face to display confidence, power, authority, and professionalism to the people who mattered most—the jury.

I tell this story to my classes because it helps people realize that even if you're in a situation where you are nearly overwhelmed with panic—which I most certainly was—you can avoid revealing your anxiety with just a bit of strategy and planning. You have yet another versatile way to tune into your natural instincts and channel them into better applications of the New Body Language. When you're especially nervous or if you have social anxiety, hold your meetings or first dates in a place where you can conceal some of your nerves under the table—a restaurant, a conference room table, behind a desk.

To cover the "bits" and other lower extremities, or not to cover them, is ultimately up to you. But the key is to be aware of how that decision can help or hurt your interaction with the person in front of you. I'd say that unless your livelihood, family life, or well-being is in jeopardy, you must learn to be cautious about subconsciously or intentionally covering up your naughty bits and locking up your legs. You might be sending the message to others that you're defenseless or edgy or feel devalued.

Ironically, many people stand this way in group photos. You can even catch some news anchors, celebrities, and an occasional politician posing this way for their publicity pictures. Their hands hang in front of them in the fig leaf position, or they clutch their wrist for dear life. This pose truly lacks power, authority, and confidence, and it always surprises me when I see powerful people standing this way. If you must do something with your hands to calm down your shyness or social anxiety, interlace them behind your back so no one can see them. (*Caution:* This move could make you actually appear superior and slightly arrogant. But since now you're using the New Body Language to get what you want in life, it's definitely the better of the two options!)

USE YOUR KNEES, PLEASE

Your knees are good for more than just self-defense. Studies have shown that touching and stroking your own knee can signal sexual interest, and the knees can act like two large, leg-shaped arrows pointing at a person or object that holds your interest. Conversely, holding or covering one's knees displays feelings of anxiousness and vulnerability. Although they often work as a part of the overall legs' signals, the knees can send signals all their own.

Stand Strong When You Work the Bits

One way you can really work your naughty bits and lower extremities to your advantage is to pay attention to your leg stance. In addition to helping frame the naughty bits, your legs can help you indicate interest, power, and confidence in a different way.

The average stance for women is less than six inches between the feet and about six to ten inches for men. While this position may seem comfortable, widening the stance a bit can help you appear more powerful. Initially, widening your stance may feel unladylike or overly masculine, but those extra inches will increase your perceived confidence, not to mention your own. (*Caution:* keep soliciting feedback from a close friend—you don't want to overdo it and look like a sumo wrestler or a gunslinger in a spaghetti Western.)

Why does widening your stance help project an image of confidence? My self-defense instructor at the ATF, Special Agent Steve Bisnett, came up with a great image for his self-defense courses. Imagine two candles on a table: one is tall and skinny, while the other is short and fat. If the table is bumped, the tall skinny candle will fall over, while the short fat one will not move. Making a wider stance sends a message that, like the short fat candle, you cannot be easily pushed around. And the last message you want to send to the world is that you don't solidly stand behind your ideas or your company. Instead, widen that stance and become a short fat candle, like supermodel Cindy Crawford, whose career has had massive longevity; Elvis Presley; and Ellen DeGeneres. These powerhouse alphas have made history as alpha leaders—and if they can do it, so can you. If you notice that you're nervous or anxious and your ankles are crossed, try this—uncross your feet, put them both on the ground, and then squeeze your toes to release your anxiety. No one will know but you!

Day 3: Learn How to Work the Naughty Bits

Now that you've seen the huge range of signals that your naughty bits give off, let's give some thought to how you can get them working for you. You'll do at least two or three of these exercises today. Once you get over your initial self-consciousness, you'll see how workin' the naughty bits is incredibly fun and effective, and not at all sexual—unless you want it to be.

▶ *"Bits" and Pieces Game.* Scan through news images on the Web from the last week or so. Pick a photograph and study it carefully. What are the people saying to you without saying a word? Match images to these emotions and messages: arrogant, confident, nervous, apprehensive, or leave me alone.

▶ *Do Some Salsa Dancing.* A great example of workin' the naughty bits and other lower extremities is salsa dancing. The name *salsa* correctly describes the flavor of this dance: hot! Danced correctly, there's a lot of shaking, shimmying, and hip action going on. In the dance, the upper body remains consistently open with large, expressive gestures while the legs do most of the work. The legs themselves are usually kept at a wide stance for smooth, confident movements as well. The arms are spread out wide or are holding on to a dancing partner—all great practice for confident body language.

The body language rules of salsa dancing apply to many other styles of dance, everything from ballet to Zumba. You would never see a dancer slouching with head hung low, ankles crossed, and hands in the fig leaf position covering the bits during a performance. Your body language should be like a dancer's: confident, expressive, and graceful.

I want you to sign up for a dance class today; it doesn't matter what kind. (You too, boys!) If you say to yourself, "I don't like dancing," that's even *more* of a reason to sign up. Aversion to dance probably means that you could use a little practice with the fundamentals of body language: a wide and confident stance, unblocked bits, a pointed belly button, and the arms taking up space. Take at least one class, no excuses!

▶ *Wear Heels Tonight (and at Least Once a Week).* The ladies on *Sex and the City* might have been on to something. High heels can help women appear more powerful than boring old flats. The heels create an illusion of height while arching the back, elongating the legs, and improving posture. Heels strengthen the pelvic floor, so the core feels stronger, and add a swing to a woman's step. Even if you don't make heels part of your daily wardrobe, spend some time in them on a regular basis.

▶ *Put Yourself on Trial.* During ATF's Advanced Courtroom Testimony class, which I took midway through my career, an innovative ATF attorney named Jeff Cohen cleverly prepared our investigators and special agents by having them testify with no podium or table. He'd put a nonswivel, straight-back chair out six feet in front of the boardroom table. Every move we'd make, from our head to our shoulders to our knees to our toes, would be seen by the entire class as we testified about a mock case.

Use Jeff's technique to prepare for that next executive committee presentation, job interview, or blind date. You never know if you will have a safety barrier hiding your "bits" and other lower extremities—if you prepare without one, you'll be ahead of the game.

Step 1. Ask a friend to role-play with you, set up your video camera, and grab a kitchen or dining room chair.

Step 2. Have your partner sit in a comfortable chair, the couch, or even behind a table, and give him something he can look at or play with, such as your résumé, a chart from your last presentation, or even a book that he can pretend is a restaurant's menu. Make sure that he is comfortable and protected, and ask him to give you limited eye contact, cross his arms, and occasionally make faces of anger or disbelief—ask him to act disrespectful. Essentially, you want him to be the worst audience possible, so you can master the art of communicating powerfully and effectively under the direst circumstances.

Step 3. Since it's your job to put yourself out there, make certain that your chair is at least six feet away from your friend's. To increase your discomfort and anxiety, you want to be at an abnormally far distance from your role-playing partner.

Step 4. Turn on your video camera. Then begin the interview, sales pitch, presentation or speech—whatever you want to practice. Maybe it's even small talk.

Step 5. Watch your performance and notice any negative behavior. Start the process over, repeating until your friend is convinced that you rocked it!

The result? By practicing Jeff's exercise you'll no longer be hiding behind jumpy gestures when you need confidence the most. Your body language will naturally be more fluid, convincing, and powerful, even when you are sitting behind a table or on the witness stand.

Name: Valerie Palmer
Age: 33
Occupation: Schoolteacher

What was holding you back? I have always felt so awkward meeting new people and going to any functions alone. I'm terrible at confrontation, sticking up for myself, asking for and getting what I want, and dealing with negative people. I've been diagnosed with an anxiety disorder, which made most social situations awkward. I never knew how to "shoot the breeze" when meeting people for the first time—I sometimes had a hard time making small talk with people I knew. My anxiety caused me many days of tears and worries. I longed to learn how to calm down and put my best face forward, and I knew the only thing stopping me was me!

How have you changed? Before doing my 7-Day Body Language Makeover, I never knew that people have a preference for either the right or left side of their body. When I greeted people at social functions, I felt awkward, nervous, and intimidated, and I tended to turn my body to the left—even if the person talking to me was on my right! I always felt as if my space had been invaded.

Now, however, I know to meet and greet new people by positioning them to my left. Using the New Right Side Rule, I make sure that whomever I am speaking with is on my left side, as I look and feel more comfortable, confident, and in control that way. When I go to dinner, I have my date sit to the left of me; when we watch a movie, I sit to his right. When I talk with coworkers, I slide up to them on their right, my left. I am better able to relax and think clearly, and I smile and laugh more. When guys see this, they laugh and smile, too.

Before the makeover, I found it very difficult to initiate conversations with people I did not know. Not now. I feel so comfortable that I initiate a friendly, "Hi, I'm Valerie. What brought you to this place?" or "How do you know so and so?" I've done a complete 180 and I feel like the Queen of Networking. Thanks, Janine, for all of my new dates!

FIVE

Day 4: Move to the Right Side

> Things are not what they seem; or, to be
> more accurate, they are not only what
> they seem, but very much else besides.
> —ALDOUS HUXLEY (1894–1963), "MAN AND
> REALITY," IN Vedanta for the Western World,
> Edited by CHRISTOPHER ISHERWOOD

Brightly colored neon signs adorned the dusty, cluttered windows, and its sills were lined with vintage guitars, used hammers, and an endless assortment of preowned pistols, revolvers, rifles, and shotguns. My time spent in the cramped pawnshop, which was located in a high-crime area twenty-five miles outside of Hartford, Connecticut, began courtesy of a firearms trafficking investigation.

Having done my homework on the owner, I knew that he was going through a divorce. Court documents showed that his wife was trying to take him for every penny he had, poor guy. One of my friends was getting divorced at the time, so I could relate to what was happening to him. During one of our first conversations, we talked about how devastating divorce could be. As I usually did with new suspects, I used the Belly Button Rule religiously, keeping my belly button pointed toward him at all times, so he would know I thought he was important. With common ground established, we quickly developed rapport and chatted like two friends over coffee. When I stood to his left side, he would take a deep swallow and put his hands in his pockets, but when I stood to his right side, he'd relax, talk more, and use his hands to express himself. Over the next few days, he would offer me donuts in the morning and pizza at lunchtime (which I would always politely refuse).

One of my primary duties was to check his "bound book," a record of his inventory, sales, and similar paperwork. I took a random inventory of the guns in the shop, finding only two types of discrepancies in the bound books: forms that were not completely filled out and entries that had been made a day or two after the transaction had occurred.

As the investigation was coming to a close two weeks later, I confronted the owner about the minor discrepancies. I could see from his shrunken posture and the fact that he covered his naughty bits that he was very uncomfortable, out of proportion to the few violations I'd found. When he talked to me, he covered his stomach with a book and crossed his arms. *Hmm*, I thought. *There's obviously more to this story.*

The day after our discussion, I arrived at the shop at 7:00 A.M. to find the owner adding entries to over twenty bound books, noting in previously empty spots that some guns had been, as he put it, "Taken back by owner." From our previous, more cordial conversations, I believed that he preferred people standing on his right side. I went to his right, kneeled down below his level, and asked, "What's going on, Ralph?"

"I forgot these people had taken their guns back," he said, not looking at me.

"Not a problem," I replied. "How do you remember that they took them back?"

"By memory." His voice was clipped and tight.

"How many years does this go back?" I kept my tone curious, not accusatory.

"Around six." He told me that he had been up all night making changes to his books.

"Not a problem," I said again, minimizing the severity of the situation. "I'm terrible at balancing my checkbook—I forget to make the entries, so I can totally relate. [Remember, people like people like themselves.] By the way, can you initial and date all the changes that you made to the books?"

He sighed.

I instantly stood up and moved to his left side, crossed my arms, angled my belly button away from him, deliberately breaking rapport, as if I were a mother disciplining my teenage daughter. I said, "Ralph, I need you to initial and date these." This time, he complied.

He made the changes over the next several hours throughout all the bound books. ATF investigator Neal Earl arrived an hour later, and the two of us conducted a full check of the store's inventory. We determined that over seventy guns were missing and that around a hundred more, which had been noted as "Taken back by owner," were still in the shop. This is a major indicator of firearms trafficking.

The following day, I woke up back at home at 9:00 A.M. and turned on the television. Breaking news: a building was on fire, and it looked awfully familiar. The pawnshop.

Somehow the bound books had wound up on a shelf next to explosive black powder, which had regrettably exploded, destroying all thirty books of records. The next day, the owner claimed insurance on some of his most expensive guns.

A few months later, police received reports that the owner was illegally selling guns out of his home. After obtaining a search warrant, they discovered that many of the guns reported as destroyed in the fire or returned to owner were sitting in his basement.

He was arrested and charged with insurance fraud. To the horror of the owner and his attorney, the signed approval and photocopies that I had made of his records helped to convict him of the crime. He was found guilty and today is a convicted felon. Not only can't he sell guns, he can't even own one legally.

My training had taught me that there is a time and a place to build rapport—and to break rapport. This experience only further convinced me that you can turn rapport on and off with one simple switch: the New Right Side Rule. Now let's learn how you can use it, too.

Accuracy: The New Right Side Rule

Have you ever been with someone whom you usually enjoy spending time with, but suddenly and for no reason, you find yourself in a bad mood when you're around him or her?

Or maybe you have arrived at meetings early so you can sit to the left side of your supervisor, but your boss always turns the other way for advice and gives you the cold shoulder?

Or perhaps you've gone on a promising dinner date, but after you were seated, the guy on the other side of the table seemed distant, closed, and standoffish?

The truth is, either one or both of you is most likely sitting in the wrong seat. Every person has an on/off switch for rapport, a "right" or more open side of her body. Knowing which side of a person's body is more comfortable for her, and which side makes her uneasy, can make for really effective body language. Believe it or not, just knowing this one truth may help you get what you want when you want it, without the other person being any the wiser.

MAGIC MIND TRICKS
OF LAWYERS AND TEACHERS

When a lawyer wants jurors to listen to a friendly witness, she'll position herself at the far end of the jury box, forcing the witness to look straight at the jury and speak loud enough for everyone to hear. Great speakers and educators, from Jack Canfield to Oprah, use this same strategy. If they ask a student a question and the student is a soft talker, the instructor will move to the opposite side of the room, so the student will have to project his or her voice.

On the other hand, during harmful testimony, lawyers study their files or consult with their cocounsel to indicate a total lack of interest. This skill is called *misdirection* and it's a mind trick that magicians use to hide what's right in front of your eyes. ○

I first began to learn about this particular body language instinct during basic training at the ATF. We learned lots of dry, boring stuff about alcohol manufacturers and importers, firearms, explosives, laws and regulations, courtroom testimony, and ethics. We also got a three-and-a-half-day course on interviewing, which was fascinating. As part of the unit on establishing rapport—my favorite part—we were taught a principle that we'll call the "Old Right Side Rule." If ever there were an example of the limits of the Old Body Language, this would be it.

This rule derived from an absolute faith in the positive power of a handshake. The theory went that when we first meet a person, our handshake becomes an anchor, a meaningful touch that creates a long-lasting emotional memory. Anchors are believed to send overwhelming signals to the brain, bypassing rational thought, allowing us to get into a certain state of mind. When we establish a positive anchor with our first handshake, the theory went, we could retrigger the anchor simply by standing on the person's right side, and he or she would unconsciously reexperience that first positive emotion. Still with me?

As a result, our instructors advised us to always stand on the interviewee's right side when he was being cooperative and honest. This technique was expected to further establish rapport and build trust with the interviewee. When the interviewee closed down or began to be deceptive, we were instructed to move to his left to break rapport, which would increase his stress and anxiety levels. The theory held that he would then begin to tell the truth in order to restore the lost rapport, because all people feel more comfortable when they are in sync with others, especially during high-stress situations. Our instructors told us that ATF inspectors and special agents used this tool on master manipulators and liars, moving from the right side to the left side during an interview to increase the pressure to be honest, to get them back on the road to telling the truth.

Sounds great, right? Well, in theory, sure. Unfortunately, the formula was flawed. But I wouldn't find that out until eleven years later when I was an instructor at that same academy, during the summer of 2004. It would take me that long to find out that our "right," or positive, side has *nothing* to do with what hand we used to shake hands, and nothing even to do with being right- or left-handed.

Reveal the Real "Right" Side

Within my first ten years with the bureau, I had already conducted more than two thousand interviews using the techniques learned from my initial basic training courses and with additional advanced training. I noticed that some tools worked with great precision, while others, like the Old Right Side Rule, only occasionally proved fruitful. Thankfully, what I lost in time with the old rule, I later made up for in efficiency with the new one.

In the summer of 2004, I was invited to teach an interviewing block to ATF's new hires. I had taught this course numerous times since first taking it in 1993. The program was interactive, playful, and always captured the students' attention. On the first day of class, everyone learned how to establish rapport and baseline the interviewee. On day two, we watched and analyzed the subtle nuances of notorious law enforcement cases from the past decade, such as the O. J. Simpson murder trial, the Tonya Harding/Nancy Kerrigan scandal, and Timothy McVeigh's Oklahoma City bombing.

After decoding the potential signs of deception, I chose several students to sit on the hot seat, a tall barstool placed in the center of class, to put their newfound skills to the test. I decided I would interview the first student on the hot seat before the class would take its turn. I asked simple rapport-building questions—How is your day going? Tell me about the first place you lived away from home. How do you like Georgia? What was your best friend when you were eight like? Tell me about the first bike you ever had—so that the student had no reason to be deceptive or anxious about answering. While I asked and he answered, I stood on the student's right side, just as I had been taught and just as I had taught every student in all of my classes for years.

On this particular afternoon, however, the feisty young woman in the hot seat immediately got angry and defensive. She crossed her arms, turned her belly button toward the door, and gave me the cold shoulder. She stated without looking me in the eye, "I do not like you on my right side!" At first I laughed, but she did not relent—she was serious. I moved to her left side and she relaxed. I was truly amazed. My faith in the Old Right Side Rule took a serious hit at that moment.

After a break, and a few minutes of careful thought, I decided to do something different.

I created an exercise right then to test my new theory. Everyone got a partner. One at a time, one of the partners walked up to his or her teammate's right side and said something like, "Jeff, I need you to repay the money I gave you." Then he or she would move to the opposite side and ask the same question. Next they would switch and the other partner would repeat the exercise.

I took a vote. Although 60 percent of the people liked people on their right side, 40 percent liked people on their left.

Since that day I have had more than twenty thousand people do this same exercise with revealing results: law enforcement officials overwhelmingly choose their gun side (often their right) as their negative side; only 20 percent choose it as their positive side. Among non-law-enforcement officials, people seem to be divided 50/50, with half the people favoring those on their right side and the other half favoring their left.

In the months following that mind-shifting seminar, I volunteered to update the lesson plans to include this information about the New Right Side Rule. This revelation became a permanent part of the lesson plans for ATF's basic training, as well as integral to techniques for Advanced Interviewing, of which I later became program manager. No matter where my body language training and analysis take me, I continue to see this rule repeated over and over. Now you too can use the New Right Side Rule to help you expand your expertise in reading people, establishing rapport, and obtaining the truth.

Testing Others' Right/Left Preference

Now that you're all pumped up about the New Right Side Rule, you want to find out what side people prefer you on, but you don't know how to go about doing it. Sometimes the direct approach is best—just ask (such as at a restaurant or at a movie, you can ask the person you're with if he has a seat preference). But if that seems too bold for your liking, try a more subtle approach. During your conversation, start on one side of the other person, then nonchalantly move to the other. If you're standing on individuals' bad side, you might see these body signs: they take deep swallows, they nervously giggle, their chin pulls in, their eyebrows suddenly dip down and in toward the bridge of the nose, their navel is redirected away from you, they cover their bits, or they put their hands in their pockets. And the opposite is true when you are standing on their good side: people relax, their arms and hands can be seen, and they may even take up more space by putting their hands on their hips. When you stand on that side, you subconsciously give them a confidence boost. Some helpful tips for getting it "right":

- Always start by putting a person on *your* good side for thirty seconds to two minutes to determine if your sides are compatible, which is not necessary to build rapport, but it deepens it faster that way.
- Then put the person on your negative side and see how his demeanor changes. When on each side, pay close attention to the flow of your conversation, the nonverbals, and ask yourself, "Does he show a special interest in having a conversation with me when I'm on his right side or his left side?" Once you determine his favorite side, stay there for five to ten minutes, then test the other side again for fifteen to thirty seconds. Anytime you make a transition—you grab a napkin, a drink, a glass of water, you step away for a phone call or a bathroom break—use each of these transitions to test the right side. Pick what you think is the best side for you to stand on, based on the intended outcome of the interaction.
- Observe how the person acts around her friends, other coworkers, and the boss—she might put people on her right side 90 percent of the time for a reason. Maybe the 10 percent is out of her control because a more alpha leader puts her on that side.

- Does he lean toward you and/or touch you subtly, such as with a pat of your hand or shoulder or upper back when you are on one side and not the other?

Once you know a person's right side, you can use it in many powerful and persuasive ways.

DETECTING RIGHT SIDE CUES

As you test for a person's "right" side, look for these cues.

- **Good Side Cues:** Shows wrinkled crow's-feet around the eyes; keeps head straight or tilted to the side; speaks in a normal tone of voice with no additional umms, errs, "you knows," or other verbal fillers; keeps chin straight or slightly tilted up with the head slightly tilted back; three power zones (throat, belly button, and naughty bits) are open; relaxes shoulders and leans toward you; hands by his side, or on his hips, or if his hands are in his pockets he is either hooking or displaying his thumbs; he uses open-palm gestures that face up; his belly button follows you when you move to this side; both of his feet point to you, or if sitting, he may sit in the figure four with the top leg the farthest away from you (to keep you in his circle of trust).
- **Bad Side Cues:** Wrinkles his forehead or smirks, sticks his tongue out a bit momentarily, bites the inside of his cheek; has trouble speaking (stutters, repeats question, has pauses that don't belong in the response), uses jumbled words when talking to you, voice lowers and is almost inaudible; grabs his own throat, raises his shoulders, crosses his arms, suddenly leans away from you, grabs his wrist; submerges hands into his pockets with his thumbs inside, fingers are clenched or palms are down; turns his belly button away from you; crosses his ankles, moves one foot angled toward a door or an exit, or if sitting, he may cross his legs or sit in the figure four with the top leg closest to you (to make a wall between you and him). ○

7-SECOND FIX

The Right Stuff

The Problem: Your gal pal is not happy, *and* you're standing on her bad side. Don't put your tail between your legs too quickly. Women don't find men who shrink away too easily all that attractive (as seen in the photo on the left); this sends the message that you lack confidence.

The Fix: Confident, even though he's still in trouble. Moving away from his wife's right side, which is her negative side, lowering his body below her eye level, and mirroring her body language helps him maintain his confidence while helping her get over her grudge a lot faster! Crafty and cunning—nice!

Application: Using the New Right Side Rule

When someone tells you not to get on her bad side, you should take it literally!

At one mother-daughter event, I taught an exercise to the six-hundred-plus attendees to help them determine their own right side. Both groups attending the event gained a valuable tool that day: the daughters knew what side to stand on when asking their mothers for keys to the car, and the mothers knew which side to stand on when asking their daughters where they would be going.

Less than a month later, one of the mothers from the event sent me an e-mail. Her relationship with her husband (physically and emotionally) had gone downhill since their early courtship, so after the class, she had decided to try out my rule with him. She changed the sheets and had them sleep on opposite sides of the bed. He was intrigued. (And by "intrigued," I'll refer you to the previous chapter, "Work Your Naughty Bits.")

This change may not sound revolutionary. But consider that she discovered that she prefers people on her right side, and her husband had been sleeping on her left side for years. Literally overnight, they reconnected with each other, got a major boost in the bedroom, and had an improved relationship with the rest of their family, too.

The New Right Side Rule crosses into all aspects of our lives, from work to recreation to our friends and family. When you're late to a meeting and are forced to sit on your least favorite side, you might actually learn less and get bored more easily. Personally, I need my husband and son to be sitting on my right side when we go to the movies. If anyone is on my left side, I feel suffocated, so I sit with the aisle to my left.

The key to maximizing the success of this rule is awareness. When you randomly put people on one side of your body without thinking anything of it, you increase your anxiety level. Maybe it wasn't the teacher's, the students', or the classroom's fault that you didn't like the class—maybe it was *yours* for not knowing your good side from your bad. When you pay attention to where you like people to approach,

MAKE YOUR MARK

If you've normed a coworker, manager, or sales prospect with his or her right side, don't forget it—put an L or an R in a notebook or on a folder to make sure you sit on that person's correct side the next time you get together.

you'll have the power to make every moment you spend with others as valuable as possible.

Making the New Right Side Rule Work for You

Becoming aware of which side of your body triggers a negative response will significantly weaken its impact and power over you. You can learn to manage that negative feeling (or "anchor," as we'll discuss in Chapter 8) and become more in charge of yourself and your moods. In a significant way, this tool helps you take charge of your life—*you* can decide you've had enough of being at the mercy of this old programmed response.

Imagine you arrive at a bar before the friend you're meeting. Two empty seats are at each end of the bar—which one do you go for? Are they the seats that put all the strangers to your positive side? If not, why? Use this rule to get what you want—even if that is to simply be comfortable around strangers.

Once you study a person and learn his or her good side, you can use it to influence the outcome of the situation. When you want to underscore rapport and continue to cooperate, position yourself on the person's positive side, especially if you're asking for a favor. If people are being deceptive, move to their negative side. It's that simple: everyone wants to be in rapport, even liars, and the uneasiness of the situation will nudge them to reveal more to the story.

Using the New Right Side Rule is a great way to gain more confidence, communicate more clearly, and have better relationships. But one caution: when you work your New Body Language magic and choose to place people on your more vulnerable side to make *them* more comfortable, make sure that your own confidence doesn't disappear. The decision is always yours: your confidence versus their comfort. Use the rule long enough, and the two will be one and the same.

Day 4: The New Right Side Rule

The purposes of today's exercises are, first, to make you aware of how you position yourself and, second, to remember to norm people's right and left side preference. Shoot for at least six, three men and three women (including kids).

▶ *Confront Your Side.* To discover the truth about which side is your "right side" when influencing the outcome of your conversation, meeting, negotiation, confrontation, or job interview, complete the test I gave the ATF trainees. Have someone come up to each side with an intense and almost angry tone of voice and demand something from you, such as, "Can I see you a minute in my office? Look at me when I am talking to you! You think it's funny?" Pay attention to how you respond. Do you pull back or wrinkle your nose when she is on one of your sides? Do you turn your head toward her, but face your belly button away from her on one side and not the other?

▶ *Gauging Your Own Side.* To use the rule effectively, you have to know your own side. Sit down and imagine yourself in each of these scenarios—where would you choose to put your body? Collect the information and see if any patterns emerge.

- **On the Plane:** If you could choose any window seat that you wanted on your next flight, and you choose to have a stranger sit to your right, while the window is to your left, maybe you're preferred side is your RIGHT SIDE.
- **On the Bus:** When you go on a bus and there are numerous empty seats (and no crazy people you are trying to avoid), you always sit in the front with your right side closest to the door, and your left side facing the passengers on the bus. Perhaps your LEFT SIDE is your comfort side.
- **At the Movies:** Each time you go to the movies or the theater with a friend or loved one you always prefer the aisle seat with the left of your body next to the aisle and your right side next to your date. And if your date happens to be sitting to your left, you immediately feel suffocated, overpowered, and you get fidgety, and the movie seems like it's never going to end. Then most likely your favorite side is your RIGHT SIDE.

- **In the Kitchen:** You're making a big dinner tonight and your wife's friends from work are coming over. As you're cooking your famous stir-fry, your wife peeks over your right shoulder and says, "Yum, everything smells delicious." But inside you want to scream, "GET OUT OF THE KITCHEN WHILE I'M COOKING!!" A couple minutes later your wife returns for another quick sniff, but this time she's on your left side. Again she commends you on your gourmet cooking skills. This time you smile and are glad she's there. This would be a great indicator that you prefer people on your LEFT SIDE.

- **In Your Office:** If your office is big enough to move your furniture around, and you've created a path for people to approach you on your right, perhaps that's your favorite side. Or, if your furniture can't move because you either have a small office or your phone and Internet cables are on the right side of your desk, do you compensate by turning your body when people walk behind your desk so that your guest is directly in front of you? Then your favorite side is certainly your RIGHT SIDE.

▶ *Sleep and Learn.* Do you like people on your right, but when you sleep with someone the person is on your left side, but it doesn't matter because you actually sleep on your stomach, which then places him or her on your good side? Just for tonight sleep on the opposite side of the bed. See what happens.

▶ *Retake Driver's Ed.* Close your eyes and think about whether or not you prefer to be the driver or the passenger. For instance, do you like driving when you're alone, but if someone else is with you in your car, would you rather ride shotgun? Is it because you like to check e-mails on your iPhone or BlackBerry? Or because you feel like you are being pampered? Or do you happen to like it better when people are on your left side? If you are a "lefty" and you find yourself uncomfortable driving when someone is sitting on your right, perhaps this feeling or anxiousness has to do with your side preference. If that's the case, just having this newfound knowledge will decrease your stress when driving with a passenger.

▶ *See Their Side.* Observe side preferences of people interacting in a crowded setting: mothers with children, people on a date, or coworkers waiting to get seated for lunch. Make a list in your Body Language Success Journal of the important people in your life. What side do you think they prefer? Take all the criteria noted from page 107 and put them in two columns (Good Side/Bad Side), then put a check mark or circle each of the displays that each of the people you're observing subconsciously leaks out. Then guess their side preference.

▶ *Be Star Struck.* Write down the name of three to five of your favorite celebs or politicians, then visit Google, click on images at the top, and see if you can determine their side preferences. Are they more often than not on the right or left side of others? And is it because that's their favorite side or their mate's favorite?

SIX

Day 5: Tune Up Your Power Gestures

> Many highly intelligent people are poor thinkers. Many people of average intelligence are skilled thinkers. The power of the car is separate from the way the car is driven.
>
> —*EDWARD DE BONO (1933-), CRITICAL THINKING EXPERT*

Coca-Cola is pretty confident about its brand. In every advertisement on television or in print, you can see that the company knows what it means to stand up and be proud.

This creative company recently held a training session to inspire its already superconfident senior-level executives to raise the bar that much further. The session challenged these execs to learn from trapeze artists, firefighters, and some of the world's most courageous and confident individuals.

As one of the trainers that day, my mission was to educate and energize this elite team to try some new body language strategies (many of which are found in this book) to take their already impressive success and give them an extra edge over their competition.

Before my presentation started, my booking agent and I were greeted by Matt, an employee with the training company that organized the event for these executives. Matt was the person responsible for booking me for the speaking engagement, and I was thrilled to meet him in person.

As a body language expert, I've gotten used to the fact that when people meet me for the first time, especially at a seminar, they think I'm going to analyze their every move and somehow read their deepest,

Name: Loretta Duverney
Age: 43
Occupation: Dentist

What was holding you back? I've been told that I have a stern look, but I really don't see that in myself. I enjoy getting out and meeting people. My favorite social activity is going to street festivals; I like mingling with people, listening to music, shopping and drinking—all in one. I'm a joker and don't take things very seriously. I'm looking for a long-term stable monogamous relationship, and I've gone to group social activities, taken art classes, gone to bars and parties. I don't know why I haven't found a relationship. I think my body language may have been sending the wrong messages.

How have you changed? By participating in the makeover, I learned that people's perception of me can be influenced by my facial expressions, hand gestures, and posture. I had been repeatedly told that I have a very stern or serious appearance, which bothered me because if someone had actually spoken with me they would have found that I am quite the opposite! I now notice that when I am out shopping or just out for a walk that if I am smiling, people smile back and some will say hello. I have become more aware of how my facial expressions influence the way people interact with me.

I also learned that I was giving people the impression I was uncomfortable with a situation when I would constantly touch my hair, face, or any other part of my body, that it looked like I needed to reassure myself. I learned that a good way to let people know you are comfortable and self-assured is to use the okay sign in a subtle manner, by resting your hand on your leg with your index finger and thumb touching.

As for my professional life, a light went on for me. A number of times while I was working with patients, they would stop me and ask if anything was wrong. I was really curious why they asked that, until I realized that when I was really focused on something, my eyebrows would contract in a microexpression of anger or stress. My patients were reading this as something was wrong or that I was upset about something. Now that I am aware of this, I tell my patients about it before I get started so they are not alarmed when it happens. I don't need to contribute to their anxiety. No one wants an angry dentist!

darkest private thoughts. It never fails—I'll shake someone's hand and then watch them close up their bodies with crossed arms, small stances, or, as in Matt's case, hands and thumbs buried deep inside pant pockets, all to prevent me from reading their minds. (I want to say, "Hey, guys? I'm good, but not that good. All you're telling me is that I make you nervous!")

My first job with anyone is to help him relax and to establish rapport. So I asked Matt questions like, "Do you like your job?" and "What do you like about it?" He began to relax. Within a few minutes, he became more confident. As he chatted about the awesome people he worked with, his interesting projects, and the company's funky office space, Matt used lots of open-palm gestures and was engaging and full of life. When he was done speaking, he put his hands back in his pockets—but this time, he hooked his thumbs, a gesture that you now know sends a message of power, individuality, and confidence. We were now in rapport and his body language had become more secure. His hands remained in that position for another ten minutes or so as we discussed the customized program I was about to present to his company's client.

Just then, a fortysomething man with an English accent bounced over to introduce himself. He explained that they were running twenty minutes behind schedule. As the man spoke, Matt got small again; his shoulders pulled forward and his thumbs snuck back into his pockets. When the snappy Brit finished his brief conversation and sprinted back to the training room, I turned back to Matt and said, "That man is either your boss or he's your superior, isn't he?"

Matt looked genuinely confused. "Yes. He's one of the two leaders facilitating the event this week," he said. "How did you know he was above me?"

"Your body told me!" I said. I explained to Matt the ways his body language had very subtly changed when the older man had joined our conversation.

Matt was genuinely dumbfounded—he had no idea his gestures had changed so much. (Little did he know when he booked me for a seminar on confidence, he'd get a miniseminar of his very own.)

Like Matt, whether we know it or not, we all use gestures to telegraph our feelings. Gestures are like the punctuation we put on our speech. Whether we are passionately defending a decision to others, drawing in the air to explain something that we dreamed, or simply waving good-bye, we use gestures consciously and unconsciously to give our verbal messages added merit.

Remember that I said we get smaller when we're nervous and bigger when we feel more confident? Gestures are how we display those changes. We shrink into nervous gestures when we're with someone we feel is more powerful, and expand our bodies with power gestures when we feel more confident.

Knowledge of gestures and what they mean is especially valuable in situations where you might need that extra bit of leverage, such as negotiations. Once you've accurately normed someone and watched him go from a powerful to a nervous gesture, you've just been granted an extremely valuable Probing Point—if you play your cards right at that moment, you might get just the piece of critical information you desire.

But my favorite use of powerful gestures is to *give you* confidence. Like Matt, we've all felt threatened, and our body language has gone from confident to closed up without even realizing it. That's why after we learn to accurately read power gestures, I will teach you how to apply your newfound knowledge to consistently send signals of strength. Power gestures not only inspire confidence in your boss without threatening him, they also make *you* feel confident and take you a good way toward that all-important attitude necessary for success.

Accuracy: Read the Gesture Continuum

Some gestures, like biting or picking at your nails, are always weak. You're not likely to see a successful corporate executive bite his nails during a meeting. Imagine Donald Trump gnawing on his fingernails during a negotiation—you just will never see it. Other gestures, like flipping the bird, are about as in-your-face as they get. But these two signals are the far ends of the continuum. There's a vast universe of nonverbal information available between the two ends of this continuum, and all of it can help you make a more accurate assessment of someone's state of mind.

Now, let's tune up your body language radar with a thorough look at the most common gestures we make, moving from weakest to strongest. You have to know where you've been to know where you're going—to the top, baby!

Weakest: Self-Touch Gestures

Self-touching signals nervousness, a lack of confidence, or even boredom. Self-touch gestures, which some body language experts call "manipulators" or "pacifiers," happen when one piece of our body touches another part of our body in an effort to soothe or calm ourselves. It's as if we are saying to ourselves, "It's okay, you can get through this."

Self-touching signals include:

- Rubbing fingers or hands together
- Fidgeting
- Picking at nails
- Rubbing arms
- Touching legs
- Putting hands in pockets

You'll often see self-touch gestures in situations that are awkward, unfamiliar, or high stress. For example, take a look at this photo.

With the amount of self-touching going on, these people are likely either very sad or very shy.

If the people in the photo were friends at the funeral of a loved one, all this self-touching would make sense. They're grouped together to console one another, but the enormity of the situation makes them self-touch as well.

On the other hand, if the people in this photo are a bunch of young business professionals at a networking event, they have a lot of work to do. All this self-touching screams insecurity, a lack of confidence, and may even send the message, "Don't talk to me—my insecurity will eventually drive you nuts!" With this body language, you're not likely to score any points with potential contacts.

As I mentioned earlier, a very common self-touch gesture is to stick your thumb inside your closed fist during times of anxiety. Even people whom you might not consider anxious types can retreat into this type of gesture at a stressful time. In the book *Life with My Sister Madonna*, Christopher Ciccone comments on how he could read his ultraconfident sister's nonverbals: "Like our father, a man of few words, neither of us have any use for small talk, as we know each other's glances and gestures by heart and can decode them with unerring accuracy. So that when my sister places her hands on her hips, fishwife style, I know there's trouble. When she starts picking on her nail varnish, usually red, I know she's nervous. And when she tucks her thumb into her palm of her hands and wraps her fingers around it . . . I know she needs reassurance."

Our bodies have three vulnerable areas: our neck dimple (the fragile indentation at the front of the neck, below the Adam's apple), our belly button, and our "naughty bits." Sometimes when people, especially women, get nervous or feel threatened, you can spot them covering their throat and their neck dimple. This self-touch gesture is a deeply unconscious instinct to protect our brains from harm. The carotid and vertebral arteries pass through the neck to supply blood to the head and brain. When we sense a threat, even a verbal challenge, we may automatically cover our throat, as if we were preventing a life-threatening attack. This move can send the message that "I don't like what you just said," "I don't trust you," "That's making me uncomfortable," or even "I'm wrong and you're right, and I'm embarrassed."

Occasionally, self-touch gestures can be appealing and attractive. A finger to the lips, caressing a leg, playing with a charm on a necklace—all are great ways women can use self-touch to draw attention to themselves.

Let's say you've normed someone who doesn't normally self-touch. If you see her doing a self-touch move, you've hit a Probing Point, the gold mine of body language. Something that was just said or done makes this person very uncomfortable; now you just have to figure out what *it* is. (We'll talk more later about how you can further capitalize on that moment to get to the bottom of things with the QWQ Formula Method in Chapter 8.)

As you watch these moves in other people, you can see how much they kill personal power, right? You don't want that. Eliminating self-touches will keep you focused and alert. And when you remove self-touch, more confident gestures and body language—straighter posture, more serene arm positions, more solid leg placement—naturally replace them. Not only will you become more focused and confident, others will see it, too. Whenever you catch yourself self-touching, hide your hands behind your back, reposition them into a power gesture, begin to take notes, or just set them at your sides. But to the greatest extent possible, for your own good, please stop self-touching.

Still Weak: Shoulder Shrug

Shrugging the shoulders is a classic sign of indifference or a lack of concern; it is a wordless "I don't know" or "whatever." When someone uses this gesture while making a definitive statement, like, "I've made my decision," a lifted shoulder shows uncertainty and resignation. It also may indicate that the person is not fully supportive of what he's saying or he's at least conflicted about it.

When you spot a shoulder shrug where it doesn't belong, don't start getting aggressive and calling him a liar. Instead, make a mental note of where the shrug appeared during the conversation—what was he saying? What were the exact words and what was the context? In Chapter 8, you'll learn a series of powerful questions that will help you dig deeper into why the person in front of you is leaking doubt and uncertainty.

The shrug is one of those unmistakable signals that is hard to miss.

During Britney Spears's emotional interview a few years ago with NBC's Matt Lauer on *Dateline,* the pop princess leaked numerous shoulder shrugs when talking about the stability of her marriage, her husband Kevin Federline's affairs and wild partying, and how she felt about rumors that Kevin was running around. Five months later Britney filed for divorce.

Stronger, but Not in a Good Way: The One-Handed Broadside Display

I'm not a big fan of this move. When we put only one hand on our hips, it conveys a kind of sarcastic sass that people can use as a weapon. We use it to push away people who've come too close, to counterattack per-ceived assaults, or to simply keep people at distance.

The person who uses this pose wants to convey confidence, but in-stead, we register it as deflection and defiance. This pose is like a coiled

One hand on a hip can be seen as irreverent and disrespectful.

rattlesnake, saying, "Take one step closer and I'll attack." True confidence, on the other hand—or hip—is more like armor.

We're not afraid of being attacked because we know there's nothing that can hurt us.

If you don't want to give off a passive-aggressive vibe—bump up that one-handed broadside display a notch and move to the more confident two-handed Superman pose.

Power Gesture: The Two-Handed Broadside Display

Although there are millions of gestures we can make, power gestures not only will help you read others, but also will help you project confidence, assuredness, and power when you're talking. The two-handed broadside display, aka the "Superman pose," is the first truly powerful gesture we'll discuss here.

Sarah Jessica Parker poses with her hands on her hips in the position called the "Superman pose." (Photo by Getty Images)

With hands resting on both hips, this positive posture sends the message that a person is ready to move forward; it's the classic sign of confidence. Sarah Jessica Parker's outward-bowed elbows create a "broadside display" by visually enlarging her upper body, making it look more powerful and imposing in size. This move lets people know you are ready to take action.

Power Gesture: The Full Frontal

When our three most vulnerable areas—the neck dimple, belly button, and naughty bits—are confidently and boldly kept open, we call this powerful triumvirate the "full frontal."

If you see a person who keeps her hands at her sides or behind her back and maintains open body language during an entire interaction, you are looking at either a very confident person or a shy person who has learned to master her own body language. This pose achieves the two very important goals of most successful encounters—it makes a person seem both approachable and confident. This pose says, "I am confident. Nothing you can do could hurt me." And nothing is more attractive and influential than that degree of confidence.

We are drawn to confident people. Their belief in themselves is more attractive than perfect features or careful grooming. Confident people come across as certain and ready to take action. They instill in us a much-desired sense of security; a feeling that, no matter what happens, we can count on them to make decisions and act in a manner that produces an acceptable outcome. Confidence is magnetic, powerful, and profound. It's the calm voice amid chaos. It's the firm hand on your shoulder when you're lost in a crowd. It's what legends and leaders are made of.

When you have confidence, you believe you can achieve, acquire, or become whatever you want. Even if you don't have this confidence, power gestures can help you get it. This is where "Fake it 'til you make it" comes in. As you use these postures, even if you don't feel 100 percent confident, you elicit a different response from people. That more respectful response, in turn, strengthens your confidence, and the cycle only strengthens with time. Power gestures are a gift to yourself that keeps on giving.

Power Gesture: The Power Steeple

Think of Tony Soprano dressing down one of his men—he always uses the steeple. Steepling one's hands fingertip to fingertip is a great way for someone to indicate subconsciously that he's knowledgeable and has everything figured out. The gesture, when paired with other confident body language and words, creates a striking message of absolute belief and assuredness.

Before now, if you hadn't known about this gesture, you may have been "steepled" into doing something you didn't want to do. But once you know to look for it, you will recognize it the second it pops out in meetings, negotiations, or other high-stakes power plays.

The best time to use steepling is to lend power to your speech when making a critical point. If a person overuses this gesture, or uses it at

Oprah Winfrey confidently uses the power steeple. (Photo by Pan Media Agency/ FilmMagic)

the wrong time, we're likely to think of the person as a know-it-all or an egotist. But when used correctly, steepling is a powerful gesture that can have a great impact, not only on the audience, but also on how a person feels about himself.

A few years ago, my parents joined me on the Royal Caribbean cruise line where I had a speaking engagement. While my extroverted mom sat in the front row during my class, and volunteered for everything, my introverted dad stopped by for maybe five minutes halfway through the presentation as a show of support. So I didn't think that he had learned anything.

Over a year later, my father had to testify in a court case. Now, you probably know a man just like my dad. He's the most honorable, hard-working man you'd ever meet. He is a shy fire department mechanic who's worked two jobs his entire life. On weekends he's outside mowing the lawn and doing yardwork. He doesn't send me handwritten letters because he's not crazy about his penmanship. He isn't a Harvard scholar, and he doesn't make six figures. For a few months before Dad's testimony, he was terrified of the coming court date. He was nervous about going to a courtroom where he would be judged by snooty lawyers, the jury, and the judge.

On a visit home after the case, Dad came in and gave me a big hug. "You're never gonna believe it. I testified in court yesterday [dramatic pause] for three hours [another dramatic pause] twenty minutes," he said in his wicked awesome Boston accent. "I did this the whole time." He made a steeple. I laughed. "It's called steepling, Janine. It means confidence and authority."

I said, "Oh, yeah, Dad?"

He added, "Yeah, the lawyers didn't know what to do because I stole their move."

What my dad had learned was not just steepling. Because he believed that the gesture meant power, confidence, and authority, he began to reflect those qualities. I'll bet if you had been in the courtroom that day, you would have seen a change in Dad's tone, posture, sentence structure, and head position. Since he believed that the gesture meant power, he began to show power.

Power Gesture: The A-OK Two-Fingered Steeple

Making the "OK" gesture with one's hand can signify agreement or feelings of confirmation, but when turned into a two-fingered steeple, it typically indicates precise thought. The two-fingered steeple is best used when making an important point.

Apple CEO Steve Jobs makes a precise point with the A-OK two-fingered steeple. (Photo by Justin Sullivan/Getty Images)

This gesture can be seen in occasional self-touches (on the leg below the table), or in a quick gesture made toward another person. The gesture itself may contradict what someone is saying, an indicator that he really feels positive about something he is speaking negatively about. In 2008, when Senator Hillary Clinton was running for president, this was her go-to gesture when speaking about universal health care. It was as if she were silently saying, "Vote for me and everything will be A-OK."

Power Gesture: The Basketball Steeple

You can never go wrong with the basketball steeple. This likable, feeling-based power gesture was displayed frequently in the crime fic-

President Barack Obama evokes passion and authority with the basketball steeple. (Photo by Scott Olson/Getty Images)

tion TV series *Columbo*. At the end of almost every case, when Columbo was ready to confront and expose the perpetrator of the crime, he would make the basketball steeple, while dangling a cigarette out of one of his hands. As a result, every time he came across as sincere, kind, and confident.

If you expand the power steeple as if you were holding an imaginary basketball, you have the added effect of seeming hopeful, likable, dedicated, and firm in your convictions. This is the most powerful steeple to get others to begin to agree with you and to believe in you. It's a power move that can be used for all occasions—weddings, family reunions, motivational speeches, confrontations, and negotiations.

A few months after one of my classes, I got an e-mail from a woman attendee. She was addicted to steepling. "I used to be shy," she told me. "But after your class and learning about steepling, things have changed. Now I steeple everywhere! At work, on the subway, even at church—and now I'm more confident!"

Power Gesture: The Aggressive Handgun Steeple

When our kids argue, lie, or are sarcastic to us, it's time to bring out the most aggressive of all steeples. The handgun steeple can be seen all over the news during political season. It's usually cocked and ready to aim in boardrooms. It literally looks like a gun with the index finger ready to shoot. While the handgun steeple can be used almost as an exclamation point, putting emphasis on what you are saying or pointing out something with force, it can also shoot down someone's ideas.

A woman prepares to shoot down an approaching man she's not interested in with a handgun steeple.

Beware that using this loaded steeple may make you seem overbearing or too controlling. Use it as a powerful tool to show that you mean business, but never use it if you are working on establishing a team environment. This is my favorite move to use on a boss who is condescending or an arrogant person who thinks he's better than everyone else in the room. It's the nonverbal equivalent of saying, "Screw you!"

Power Gesture: Palm-Down Gesture

The palm-down gesture is powerful for negating and nullifying others. It often makes its debut during a handshake (as seen below left). When one person wants to clearly let the other person know that he's in charge, he will slightly twist the other person's hand into a palm-up gesture, while the person in need of power secures the top, palm-down position. You can respond to this power-hungry gesture by giving a little hand hug with your other hand. You'll neutralize his power with a touch of class. (And ladies, don't be afraid to use the upper-hand handshake when you want to let the big boys know that you will not be pushed around.)

You can come back from an overdominant handshake by giving a "hand hug."

Much in the same way that a person shows dominance by giving a palm-down handshake, gestures with hands pointed down stifle what others are saying. A person who uses a palm-down gesture indicates that he is in charge and his bidding must be done.

Not surprisingly, this gesture has a strongly negative connotation and should be used sparingly. It's incredibly handy, however, if you need to discipline your child or confront someone who is lying to you. It says, "Pay attention to me and what I have to say right now, or there *will* be consequences."

For instance, in the photo on page 130, the man on the left in the suit jacket appears to almost be reprimanding the man on the right, or

In a corporate setting, the palm-down gesture can send a signal of close-mindedness.

maybe he's pushing away his ideas, concerns, directions, or thoughts. The man on the right has his right hand in a fist, has his eyebrows pulled down in an angry and confused expression, and to top it off, his belly button is angled away from the palm pusher. Let's hope the man on the right is not the boss—if he is, the well-dressed palm pusher might be getting a pink slip during the next round of layoffs.

If a person uses this gesture in the wrong situation (such as while asking your boss if you can work from home two days a week or asking family members to lend you money), emotions may escalate quickly, causing an argument or even worse. The person may even do the *opposite* of what you'd like her to do.

If you believe that a palm pusher is pushing you around unfairly, you can either direct your belly button away from him, shoot him down with the handgun steeple, or if the palm pusher is sitting, you could stand up and bring out your inner Superwoman pose with hands on hips. Or you could simply relax, lean back in your chair, and put your hands in a steeple above your head (like a crown). This move is one of ultimate confidence, and it can anger people because you're effectively saying, "You can't intimidate me." But using this kind of nonverbal power on an overgrown bully can sometimes be a lot of fun! Bottom line: use the palm-down gesture infrequently to make a powerful statement—but be careful.

In-Your-Face Gesture: Middle Finger Displays

Many people consider "the bird" the Mac Daddy of all power gestures, and with good reason—what other single finger can provoke fistfights and murderous rages? But I'll bet if you knew how often people give you the one-fingered salute, you'd be shocked!

In boardrooms across the nation, this power gesture appears resting on businesswomen's legs and camped on the side of arrogant men's faces. During high-stress situations, the bird is the finger of choice, for both men and women, to push up glasses and scratch noses. But does its meaning change when you use your middle finger to touch your face?

A subconscious show of the middle finger can leak frustration or arrogance.

In short, yes. While a person may just be scratching an itch, a prolonged middle finger on the face can signify disagreement, dislike, or possibly hidden feelings like resentment or discomfort. In March 2004, during an episode of *American Idol,* judge Simon Cowell made the gesture to one of the other judges when he rested his head exclusively on his middle finger. He was not flipping Paula off, but he had made the gesture subconsciously as he disagreed with what she had said.

People don't always mean to flip you off; sometimes it just happens. So it's your job to find its hidden meaning (if there is any).

For instance, I had arranged to interview Lisa, a graphic designer, about working together on a project. We had previously worked together at ATF, although we weren't close, and had arranged for a brief, late-afternoon meeting to discuss the idea.

Things seemed to be going well, and we quickly built a strong rapport with each other. In fact, we ended up talking to each other for a lot longer than we had planned. Then I noticed it. To a casual observer, it might have seemed that Lisa was rubbing her nose . . . or giving me the bird! (I had the same feeling that George had in that episode of *Seinfeld* when he gets flipped off by the waitress.)

Thoughts and doubts started racing through my mind. Did she not like me? Was she uninterested in the project? Did she have no intention of following through? Was she using me for a free dinner? Or was it just an itch? I had no idea what was going on. But I decided to ask. "Lisa," I began. "I might be wrong here, but is there something that is making you uncomfortable?"

"Actually, yes," she replied. "I really enjoy talking with you, but I parked my car up the street and the meter ran out twenty minutes ago. I can stay for another hour—I just need to put more money in the meter."

Had I simply assumed that Lisa was uninterested or did not like me, the entire business deal could have been sabotaged. Instead, I noted the gesture as a departure from her norm, got to the root of the problem, and quickly resolved the situation.

We often make the mistake of assuming that a body language signal can only mean one thing. But that Old Body Language mistake has cost us in too many situations and relationships. Certain gestures *can* suggest

7-SECOND FIX

Who's Your Daddy?

The Problem: The man in these two photos is demonstrating the traditional steeple, a powerful yet controversial gesture to use if you want to inspire teamwork, comfort someone who's grieving, or are on a date.

The Fix: Transition to a basketball steeple, as it packs an authoritative yet more open and emotional punch.

specific emotions, intentions, or states of mind, but remember—we can never presume to be mind readers! Accuracy is all about the moment of *change*—and then application is about making that change work for *you*.

Application: Advanced Power Gestures

Now that you've mastered the full continuum of weak to strong gestures, it's time to move on to some advanced moves: the "grab-and-release" and "guiding." These tools are definitely not for the faint of heart. Both employ touch, which is like a gesture on steroids—and take body language into a new category altogether. Touch can be a tool for establishing rapport or destroying it, a tremendous lesson I learned one evening in a restaurant in New York City.

The Grab-and-Release

With seats for no more than fifty people, the restaurant was nestled in a trendy, bustling neighborhood on New York's Upper West Side. We had just ordered dessert and another glass of white wine when a regal older woman walked in with her quiet, beautiful, yet somewhat guarded teenage granddaughter and took a seat to my right on the same cushioned bench. She was only a half-outstretched arm away from me when I joked, "Sorry! You're *late* and we couldn't wait any longer for you to eat, so now we're on our dessert."

Despite being in her eighties, she didn't miss a beat, "I'm so sorry, but my granddaughter wanted to go back to the hotel and change into jeans. How was your meal?"

"Great!" I replied. The four of us laughed. I had no idea who the woman to my right was, but my overly friendly personality, which I inherited from my mom, was as always cocked and ready to fire.

My dinner companion slid me a handwritten note, "I think that's Cloris Leachman." After a quick peek back at the elderly woman to my right, I wrote, "Who's Cloris Leachman?" When I got the note back from my business associate this time it said, "FROM *The Mary Tyler Moore Show!*" (This was, of course, before she burst back onto the scene doing the tango on *Dancing with the Stars*.)

When I glanced back at my playful new friend on my right, I could see it was her.

A second later, she began making funny, foul-mouthed comments about the fact that the butter had no salt. I was so delightedly overcome by her moxie and quick wit that I unexpectedly assaulted her! Yes, by accident. I hit my new dinner neighbor on her upper arm, with an Elaine from *Seinfeld* violent-like push, and said with a smile, "Are you famous?"

"Yes, I am," she confidently proclaimed.

"Are you Cloris Leachman?" I asked.

"Yes, I am!" she said with pride.

How amazing! I was sitting next to one of the funniest actresses of all times, and she was so cool!

Over the next hour and a half, the four of us began chatting like old friends at a high school reunion, sharing our thoughts about how exciting New York is, about the movie Cloris was there making, and how I was going to be a guest on the *Today* show the next morning. Throughout the friendly chitchat, I would occasionally slam poor Cloris in the arm with a random, "Get out of here!" heavy-handed hit.

Finally fed up, she yelled at me with a nanalike force: "Stop hitting my arm! If you want to grab my attention or make a dramatic point, you don't hit and release like a woodpecker chopping down a tree. You grab, hold on, then you throw me away." She demonstrated on my arm.

Minutes later, by mistake, after another exciting story, I hit her again. She yelled at me yet again. "I'm so sorry, Cloris. I get the hitting from my mom. We both hit people's upper arms when we feel connected to someone. It won't happen again."

Twenty minutes later, another hit accidentally snuck out. As you can imagine, I was embarrassed. I apologized and when I did, I laid my hand firmly on her arm and held it there with the strength you'd use to move an iron across a wrinkle in your pants. Then I passionately released my hand and threw her away. (Inside I was nervously wondering if I had overdone it). "Now that's how you touch someone," Cloris cheered.

After teaching the importance of body language for a living for the past decade, it wasn't until that night that I realized how the power of touch, when used inappropriately—even with the best intentions—can break rapport.

Learn from my mistake. When you choose to touch someone while making a point, or to connect after they share with you a dramatic story, touch them solidly with passion and love, and then throw them away. The touch should be a minimum of three seconds, none of my Elaine-like battering.

Unfortunately, I admit that I still occasionally do the Elaine hit out of habit. But every time I do it now, I apologize and share with my victim all about the day I met Cloris Leachman!

A solid touch in a social situation can solidify rapport.

Guiding

Another way you can use touch to show strength and confidence is with a guiding touch. These subtle touches include a gentle hand on the back when leaving a room, walking in a hallway, and so on. Guiding touches send the signal that you know where you are going, can help lead the other person there, and have a clear direction in your actions. This also gives you power over other people as you are leading them somewhere.

When guiding someone in or out of a room or a building, make sure your hand is on his upper back in the center of his back up near and between the person's shoulder blades. All of our current living presidents love to use this move as a signal of power and connection with others. For instance, President Obama pulls out this authoritative touch anytime he's walking with another person of power. (He also uses the bicep squeeze/back pat combo while saying hello.)

If the person is a romantic interest, you can place your hand on the bottom of her back over the sacrum area just above her pants (this move will make women melt). Hold the touch for up to seven seconds, as long as you're moving toward the door or the area you're both headed and as long

THE PAUSE THAT PERSUADES

Once every thirty to sixty seconds, take a three-second pause when presenting new information. Simply think the words "three-second pause," which add up to three seconds. This will allow a listener's brain time to better assimilate new information, and you'll become a powerful presenter and leader.

as it's solid and firm—the same pressure you'd use to push your shopping cart. Be careful to use this move sparingly; it can easily be interpreted as being pushy or overbearing. Do not use it more than once on any individual over a short period of time or you might be perceived as a less powerful, "touchy-feely" person. You want your touches—like all your gestures—to communicate confidence and authority, not anxiety and supplication.

Day 5: Power It Up!

By using the various power gestures sparingly and appropriately, you can gain confidence and power in your relationship with others without saying a word. These subtle moves make you feel and appear more considerate, deliberate, and, most of all, confident. Do these exercises to help you home in on the power gestures that best suit—and help—you.

▶ *It's Showtime!* Ready for your close-up? Take out your videotape from the first day so you can see what kinds of negative moves you were unknowingly performing in your baseline body language. Were you self-touching, slouching, using a lot of ums, moving around a lot, talking fast? Take out your Body Language Success Journal—you're going to need it. Note all the "mistakes" you'd been making. You'll be amazed at how much more you can notice about your own baseline.

If you're brave enough, ask a close friend (or three) to watch the tape as well. Ask them if they can find at least three nonverbal ways that you appear to lack confidence.

▶ *Steeple People.* Pick a steeple, or try them all, and use it during a meeting, when listening, or when making a point. Go steeple crazy!

▶ *Pick Some Role Models.* Notice what powerful people whom you know do. Study their moves and match their body language to send out equally strong messages. Once you feel confident that you know their repertoire, use any of the moves outlined in this chapter to level the playing field.

▶ *Single Ladies, Take a Wrist Risk.* Once you've mastered the art of keeping your three vulnerable zones open in the full frontal pose, the next step is to make sure you relax your hands. Then muster up the courage to present yourself to your potential suitor by flashing your palms toward the person and showing your wrists.

1. Just for fun throughout today, flash your wrists at different people at work or on the street, so you can gain a better awareness of this amazing, subconscious flirting tool.
2. Notice what women you consider to have the art of flirting and sex appeal down to a science do with their wrists.
3. Take note of celebrities in gossip mags while you're waiting in line at the grocery store. Scan through pictures and notice which women expose their wrists and which ones don't. Check out Angelina Jolie—she's a great example.
4. Research has shown that men are attracted to the smells of vanilla or cinnamon. If it appeals to you, splash either scent on the pulse points of your wrists.

SEVEN

Day 6: Put Your Best Face Forward

> Emotions are shown primarily in the face, not in the body. The body instead shows how people are coping with emotions.
>
> —PAUL EKMAN (1934–), PSYCHOLOGIST AND NONVERBAL COMMUNICATION PIONEER

One dramatic yet essential function of the ATF is to make sure people who manufacture and sell guns pay their taxes correctly. When a large firearms manufacturer was believed to have underpaid its taxes in 1996, ATF senior investigator Tom Shalayda was assigned to the case. If there were an error in the records, brilliant and extremely disciplined Tom would be the one to discover it. My supervisor thought it would be a good idea for me to observe the auditing process, so for five months, Tom and I immersed ourselves in the documents of the firearms manufacturer.

At the end of the audit, Tom and I presented the president of the company with the government's tax bill. The company had accidentally miscalculated its manufacturing taxes; with penalties and interest, it owed more than a million dollars. Needless to say, the president was not pleased.

Two weeks later, Tom discovered another small error that would add approximately $2,000. When we went back to the company to explain the newfound error, the president opted not to join our meeting and asked his vice president and support staff to speak with us instead.

The employees brought us to an oblong table in an open area that happened to be situated directly outside the president's office. During

Name: Cory Laws
Age: 39
Occupation: Home Improvement Contractor

What was holding you back? I have always had good people skills, but I wanted them to be great. I'm fairly confident, but I have baggage from a rather intense upbringing and two failed marriages. I'm very interested in self-improvement in both business and personal areas. I want be able to read people better and to project an image of success and trust to increase my odds of gaining high-end clients and the lucrative contracts they represent.

How have you changed? For me, the 7-Day Body Language Makeover can be distilled down to a single word: awareness.

I've been given a code that allows me a glimpse into the inner person people choose to hide or suppress. It's a powerful thing.

I think Day 6 was the best day of the program. I have largely corrected my head posture when speaking, but the most important thing I realized is that I have to soften my image. I'm not a small guy, and with my inherent level of intensity, I can be intimidating at times.

Now, when I go on an estimate, I make a point to use good body language. People buy from people they like, and it's easier to like a smiling person than a frowning one. I carefully watch for the prospects' reactions to gauge my chances of capturing the contract. I find that the body language tools, coupled with my own sales experience, allow me to create rapport quickly, and determine whether that rapport is real or contrived.

Of late, I've been winning a larger percentage of the opportunities, for two reasons. First, I truly believe that my interpersonal skills have improved. Second, with my heightened social skills, I've become more adept at transferring my passion to my clients, who are then energized to become evangelists for me and my business. This situation builds on itself. Since the 7-day program, I've done two full kitchens (for a total of over $130K), where I'd only done two (much smaller) kitchens in the previous four years.

The training has also benefited my personal life. Whether it's a slight microexpression or a macroexpression, I'm much more aware of my personal interactions, and at least some of the psychology behind them.

When I left my marriage and started my home improvement company, I decided to surround myself with positive energy. As I've grown individually, all roles I play have benefited. I'm a better father, a better business leader, and overall a better man. And the 7-day program has proven to be the catalyst that made all this possible.

the meeting, I could see the president pacing back and forth in his office. Soon I noticed that both his left and right fists were clutched, his brows were furrowed down, and his upper lip had completely disappeared. This was much more than anger; this was rage.

I was not surprised when moments later the president threw a penny on the table and said, "Here's the extra penny you came back for, now get the fuck off my property." His blood pressure and pulse rate must have been through the roof. He hurled all rational thinking out the window and screamed at two federal officers, "I'M SICK OF SEEING YOU PEOPLE HERE. I'M GOING TO CALL MY CONGRESSMAN. GET YOUR SHIT AND GET THE FUCK OUT NOW!"

Tom and I closed our computers, said very little, and left the premises immediately.

When I look back now, I see that this situation could have been avoided if they'd chosen a more private setting for this meeting, rather than in full view of the already piqued president. I already knew to pay very close attention to extreme shifts of emotion, so when I noticed the president's anger, I should have signaled to Tom to quickly wrap up the meeting. We hadn't been thinking about the emotions of the other parties—we were just eager to finish the job we'd started five months earlier. We weren't thinking of the big picture.

Has this ever happened to you? Have you been so intent on completing a task that you missed the bigger picture—and when you look back, you see how closer attention to the emotions of the situation would have created a better outcome?

The ability to read people's facial emotions is fundamental to the New Body Language. Most of us have no trouble spotting happiness, sadness, or fear. This chapter is about how you can recognize a few of the more complex emotions on people's faces, emotions people don't always *want* you to see. You need this skill, not only to understand the needs of others (and adjust your approach to achieve what you want) but simply to stay safe!

Accuracy: Spotting the Dangerous Four

Almost anything you want to know about people can be as plain as the nose on their face. Every person has forty-three facial muscles that create the same expressions, whether we're from the western mountains of Cuba or the valleys of California.

Pioneering researcher Dr. Paul Ekman has proven that humans share seven universal emotions that trigger the same muscles in each of our faces. Early in his career, Ekman believed that facial expression was learned, imprinted upon us from our family and other social influences. But as his work progressed, he became more and more convinced of Charles Darwin's theory that the facial expression of emotion was intrinsic. In his effort to determine the truth, Ekman traveled to Papua, New Guinea. It was there that he found members of the Fore tribe, an isolated people with a Stone Age–like society and technology, who could accurately identify expressions of emotion in photographs of people they had never seen before. From this research, Ekman determined that all humans share six key emotions:

Anger
Disgust
Fear
Happiness
Sadness
Surprise

He later added a seventh, Contempt.

Anger

- Lips narrow, red part of lip rolled in tight
- Lower and upper eyelids pulled up
- Eyebrows pulled down
- May flash teeth like a growling dog ready to attack

Contempt

- Lip corner pulled in and back on one side of face
- *Note:* This is the only emotion demonstrated on one side of a person's face.

Disgust

- Upper lip pulled up
- Nose wrinkled
- Brows pulled down
- *Note:* This is often seen with just the upper lip pulled up.

Fear

- Mouth corners stretched back
- Eyelids open wide and you can literally see "the whites of his eyes"
- Eyebrows up and together

Happiness

- Both lip corners pulled up and toward the ears (vs. toward the back of the jaw)
- Crow's-feet around the eyes
- Narrow eye openings

Sadness

- Lip corners down and mouth hangs open
- Eyelids heavy
- Inner corner eyebrows turned up
- *Note:* When faking sadness, turning the inner eyebrows up is one of the most difficult movements to make.

Surprise

- Mouth hangs open
- Eyebrows up and eyelids open wide
- *Note:* Surprise is the quickest of all emotions and in less than three seconds will turn into one of the other emotions.

Each of these emotions can be clearly distinguished on the face of anyone on the planet. According to Ekman, emotions manifest themselves in facial expressions and developed as a part of human evolution—they were our way of letting others know we sensed danger.

Now, since the time of the caves, we've obviously learned a thing or two about hiding our true feelings. ("No, really, that hat looks great on you!") But we still retain certain biologically driven facial expressions that are involuntary, some of which last less than a quarter of a second. Ekman termed these *microexpressions,* and if you can learn to catch them, you'll be amazed at what they can tell you about what other people think and feel.

Because we are trusting souls, we sometimes accept the first expression people display—then feel entirely duped when they later reveal their true selves. For example, let's say that, on her first day of work, your new boss arrived with a twinkle in her eye and a smile on her face. She seemed thrilled to be part of the team and she praised the hard work you and your coworkers had done to win awards and gain recognition. But two months later, you have to drag yourself into work every day, hoping to slide into your cubicle undetected by the negative, power-hungry monster who has somehow replaced your fun-loving new boss.

What happened? How could you have known at the outset that your new boss was going to be a gigantic bitch?

One way you could have known is if you'd learned how to spot her split-second microexpressions. You might then have noticed her telling microexpression of disrespect on the first day, a fleeting half-smile, or smirk, that was actually an unmistakable expression of contempt and moral superiority. I call that expression "Killer Contempt," one of the Dangerous Four microexpressions that can signal big trouble.

What microexpressions don't tell you is *why* people are feeling a certain way, but in Chapter 8, you'll learn the secret questions to ask people to get them to tell you more than they think. Now, we'll explore how to train yourself to tune into the Dangerous Four by spotting key facial changes. Once you can identify the movements, you can get to the truth faster—and if need be start the hunt for your next job.

Spotting the Dangerous Four

For purposes of the 7-day program outlined in this book, I'm only going to introduce you to four of the seven universal emotions—all of which have a deceptive twist—in what I call the "Dangerous Four":

1. Psychopathic Happiness (also nicknamed "Duper's Delight")
2. Fleeting Anger
3. Disguised Disgust
4. Killer Contempt

To assign emotional meaning to the muscular actions of the face, it's important to first understand that face reading can be difficult: it's easy to confuse one set of signs with another. Fear and surprise, for example, share similarities: the eyebrows go up and the mouth opens in both. But research indicates that despite initial skill level, through studying and training, all of us can improve our ability to spot and crack the code for nonverbal facial communication.

With that in mind, let's take a look at each of the Dangerous Four emotions.

▶ *Psychopathic Happiness, aka Duper's Delight.* My phone began to vibrate as I walked to my midafternoon speaking engagement at the World Bank in downtown Washington, D.C. On the other end of the phone was a producer from *Inside Edition*. The show wanted to do a segment on the murder of a young mother and her nine-month-old daughter that had taken place in Hopkinton, Massachusetts, less than thirty miles from where I grew up.

The husband and father of the victims was a British-born computer programmer, Neil Entwistle. While images were shown in court of the bloody crime scene where Rachel Entwistle and nine-month-old daughter Lillian were found huddled together and shot dead, Neil partially covered his face and began to cry—at least that's what his attorney wanted us to believe—while he was perversely showing signs of joy and happiness. "There is no way that Neil would be laughing. He's grieving. He's lost his wife. He's lost his baby. You've heard what a loving father he was, what a loving husband he is," said his attorney.

Later that night, I was a guest on *Inside Edition*. After a brief video clip, I told it as I saw it. "He's [Entwistle] leaking how he is really feeling about what he is seeing," I said. "If it were just for a couple of minutes, I would say it is possible he could be nervous. But this is not sadness. A big smile on your face and the crow's-feet around your eyes—you don't have to be a body language expert to see this to know that this is not sadness. This is not grief."

What Neil's face revealed is not uncommon for criminals, especially psychopaths. Duper's Delight is an expression of joy and happiness, the delight they get out of being deceptive. The liar experiences a moment of pride and enjoyment at successfully duping the other person. So when the emotion doesn't fit the circumstances, you should ask yourself, "Why is he experiencing joy when he should be devastated?"

Check out the following photographs. One photo just doesn't belong here—which one doesn't match the others?

Left: Convicted murderer Neil Entwistle, who slaughtered his wife and nine-month-old baby daughter. Center: Hungary's Timea Toth crying after being defeated by South Korea in the women's handball bronze medal match of the 2008 Beijing Olympic Games. Right: Prince Charles, Prince of Wales, at a charity event in Hill Holt Woods on January 20, 2009, in Lincoln, England. (Photos by Getty Images)

Can you see it? The photo on the left of Entwistle doesn't fit the other displays of sadness. Entwistle is actually laughing. In true sadness or grief, the corners of our mouth are turned down, our inner eyebrows are pulled together and slightly up toward our hairline. Entwistle is demonstrating Duper's Delight.

Duper's Delight is not just reserved for murderers. Remember the bitchy boss we talked about, who had leaked Killer Contempt for you on her first day on the job? She may indeed have been smiling with true joy on her first day—but that might also have been her Duper's Delight at having received the promotion despite not being the sharpest knife in the drawer. (One way you can tell a fake smile from a real one: smiles shorter than two-thirds of a second or longer than four seconds are often false smiles.)

SURPRISE SNEAKS

In the law enforcement world, the most innocent people flash the most genuine surprise (eyebrows up and curved; mouth open and relaxed). Meanwhile, guilty people usually display a similar expression of fear (eyebrows up and straight; mouth open), but hold it for longer, which is more indicative of someone who has something to hide. So when you confront your teen about the scratch on the side of your car, or your employee about the missing petty cash, watch how the brows and mouth move, and for how long. If they demonstrate prolonged surprise, you have found yourself a Probing Point. ○

▶ *Fleeting Anger.* Most of us are fascinated by anger, and we love to watch people get angry—from a distance. From brawling hockey players, to chair throwing on *The Jerry Springer Show,* to a bald Britney Spears attacking a paparazzo's car with a closed umbrella, people seem unable to look away when they see a fight. But when it's staring us straight in the eye and moving into our personal space, a fight's not so entertaining!

Generally, people believe that anger is our strongest and most aggressive

England's David Beckham stepped into the referee's personal space (less than three feet), and leaked anger (lowered furrowed brows; open, taut mouth and jaw) as he argued. (Photo by Getty Images)

emotion. Anger is a natural emotional state that ranges from mild feelings of annoyance and frustration to full-on rage. Although some anger helps protect us from harm, we don't really need to talk about the upside of anger here; our focus instead is on its destructive side.

Expressions of anger are acceptable behavior in sports or reality TV, but displaying a lot of anger with your family or at work can be deadly to these close relationships. When anyone in your life leaks anger, a red flag should go off in your head—tread carefully.

People become quite angry for a number of reasons:

- When someone lets us down, breaks his or her word, antagonizes us, or we are otherwise lied to or manipulated
- When someone is anxious; anxiety can provoke aggression and anger more readily, because the raw emotion of anger gives nervous people a feeling of power

- When someone is an underachiever; people who underachieve and hold themselves back can get frustrated and angry easily
- When someone lies; liars often flash anger toward people who are getting closer to the truth—fearing they'll be caught, they'll use aggression to push the truth seeker away.

Others may have chronic anger problems. According to a recent Harvard study, sixteen million Americans have a mental disorder you may never have heard of: "intermittent explosive disorder," or IED. People with IED overreact to situations with uncontrollable rage, perhaps because they feel a sense of relief or release during the outburst. At the end of the outburst, they feel remorseful—but it doesn't stop the next outburst. People with IED can freak out over the smallest provocation, attacking people or things, causing physical injuries or damage to other people's possessions (road rage, anyone?). They are verbal bullies who like to threaten others, and although they are predisposed to depression, anxiety, and drug or alcohol abuse, the disorder is not caused by any of these afflictions.

Sound like anyone you know? Once you begin to notice the subtle indications of hidden anger, you'll be able to gain a deeper perspective on the situation and you'll be able to protect yourself against harm, deception, or embarrassment. Here are some rules on how to handle extreme anger when you see it.

Rule 1: If you feel or sense that you might be in for a verbal or physical attack, decrease eye contact; make your body small by covering your midsection, throat, or naughty bits; stop talking; and begin to slowly move toward an exit. Do not ask angry people why they're mad or rationalize why they shouldn't be mad—they cannot be reasoned with at this time. For example, if you detect quick-flashing subtle signs of anger (lowered furrowed eyebrows, raised upper eyelids, and thinned lips) on your boss's face when you tell her that you are resigning, the last thing you should ask her is if she is mad. This could be the catalyst for a verbal attack.

Rule 2: If you like the person, and you think an opportunity to talk might help the anger subside, try to draw the individual out a little.

(We'll talk about this technique more in Chapter 8.) For instance, if you are speaking to your four-year-old toddler and she displays anger, you might say to her, "I know that you're upset that you can't play on the swing set in the rain, and I expect you are disappointed with Mommy. Would it help to talk about it now or later?" Notice I did not use the word *angry*.

When people are angry, they may temporarily feel they can do no wrong and everything is someone else's fault. (Of course, this could apply to you, too.) If you see this pattern, tread lightly. Put yourself in the mind-set of tolerance and patience, and add even a splash of kindness. But do keep in mind there may be nothing you can say or do that will calm them down. Understand that it's not you, it's them. Above all else, keep yourself safe. And be sure to put yourself in their shoes when you're angry as well.

BE HAPPY, MAKE THE SALE

According to a recent study conducted at the University of Virginia, close friends have difficulty detecting a friend's hidden anger, but a mere acquaintance can pick up on the signs of our anger relatively quickly. Friends give us the benefit of the doubt. But with business contacts, the onus is on us. Remember: your new prospect doesn't have that much invested in you. If he senses angry microexpressions from you, even if it's about your parking ticket, he might think you're unhappy with the deal, negotiation, or project—or worse, that you're a bully. Release any hidden anger before you walk into a business meeting, or it could cost you a bundle.

▶ *Disguised Disgust.* The cousin of contempt, disgust is a powerful emotion that, left unchecked, could lead to escalating anger, feelings of hatred, or physical altercations. Disgust is indicated by a wrinkled nose; a scrunched upper lip; a contorted, tight mouth; and a shrunken face with a furrowed brow. We show disgust when we are, well . . . disgusted.

Like mother like daughter: My youngest sister, Caileen, and her middle daughter demonstrating "Disgust."

As with all body language, noticing true disgust is only possible after you've normed someone. I have an incredibly thin upper lip, so when my face is relaxed, to a stranger, sometimes I may appear angry or disgusted. When I'm going on television, the makeup artist actually has to draw me an upper lip! (Thankfully, my personality is about as far from disgust and anger as possible, so people don't hang on to that impression for very long.)

▶ *Killer Contempt.* Contempt, also referred to as scorn, is an emotion often associated with feelings of moral superiority. It appears when someone feels someone or something else is inferior or worthless. It's best characterized by a smirk (a half-smile on one side of the face). Contempt is not always an indicator of deception, but it can be a sign that someone has justified his or her actions in a way that might be seen as immoral or detrimental to others.

Contempt may often be seen in people who are pleading innocence when they are guilty, such as convicted murderer Scott Peterson. Bad guys will often unconsciously leak contempt—rather than showing concern or

---

TUBE UP YOUR DETECTION SKILLS

During an appearance on Oprah Winfrey's talk show, magician, illusionist, and stunt performer Criss Angel was able to determine which number the hostess had chosen from between 1 and 100. How did he do it? Telepathy? Precognition? X-ray vision? Magic? Hardly; he may have used microexpressions and embedded commands. Embedded commands are patterns of language that bypass conscious reasoning and speak directly to the subconscious mind.

Angel repeatedly told Oprah, *"Don't* give me any visible indications" and even told her that he was watching her patterns. He used her blinking, breathing patterns, and, finally, microexpressions of surprise—her eyebrows jumped slightly and her head moved slightly when he guessed her number. By accenting the negative command, Angel had drawn attention to the words after *don't,* which subconsciously told Oprah to give him visible indications. Much in the same way that "Don't run in the street" is less effective than "Stay on the sidewalk," embedded commands influence people at the subconscious level. (Watch the Oprah and Criss Angel clip at youtube.com by searching for "Criss Angel on Oprah 2007.")

---

shock, or what most innocent people leak, surprise—while being questioned by police, when they think they are putting one over on the person in authority. (And the bad guy can be your kid or your employee or your boss—anyone who believes he's better than you or has a leg up on you.)

According to Dr. John Gottman, professor emeritus of psychology at the University of Washington, who is best known for his research into the qualities that determine marital longevity, contempt is the grim reaper for newlyweds because it signals moral superiority. As highlighted in *Blink* by Malcolm Gladwell, Dr. Gottman can predict with 90 percent accuracy which newlywed couples will remain married and which will divorce four to six years later. The primary factor? If one of the spouses unconsciously displays contempt.

When people experience contempt, they have such a high regard for themselves, they come across as cold, arrogant, and bitchy. They

The face of Debbie Clemens, wife of former major league pitcher Roger Clemens, shows contempt during the House Oversight and Government Reform hearing on steroid use among MLB players.

typically expect someone else to remove the person or object that is causing the contempt, or they feel that the person who evoked contempt should immediately leave on his or her own. If the person or object of contempt is not removed, the person experiencing contempt will do one of two things: withdraw or approach. To be on the safe side, always prepare for the worst. Here's how to handle a few of the most problematic situations involving contempt.

ACTIVATE YOUR BRAIN POWER DURING DANGEROUS SITUATIONS

When people experience unexpected high anxiety, their thoughts bypass their higher-level rational thinking neocortex and head straight to the most primitive part of the brain, the amygdala, the seat of fear. This is why smart people often do stupid things when they are under enormous bursts of stress. Even your husband's ex-wife, or the guy whose car you just crashed into, can physically attack you for simply being in the wrong place at the wrong time! To be safe, follow these three steps

The Contemptuous One	The Fix
Teenagers	You must deal with the red flags before your tenacious teen flashes contempt. When a child becomes contemptuous, you have a very difficult situation—some parenting experts believe it's almost beyond hope. Your child basically believes you have done something so horrible that you have no value, and talking to you is a waste of breath.
	To prevent emerging signs of contempt, look for a change in behavior. Perhaps he begins to speak to you less and he spends more and more time alone in his room. Ask yourself why—what is happening in his life that is making him feel this way? Approach your son with a small stance, open palms, and put your body lower than his. Next, to understand how he's feeling, ask, "Have I done something wrong?" By taking this approach you are taking responsibility for his behavior, even if you think it's not your fault.
	If he's already reached the point of contempt, you still need to find out the cause—until you discover the cause, you can't figure out a solution. Keep your three power zones open (neck dimple, belly button, and the "bits"), sit lower than him, and share what you are feeling. "When you do this . . . it makes me feel like this . . ." Expect him to say, "Who gives a shit?" Say, "I do, and I'm really concerned."
Know-it-Alls	No matter what you do, those who think they know everything will often leak contempt. Your move should be to mirror their body language, stance, and head position. Next, acknowledge their point of view, praise them, then (and only then), say, "On this occasion, we're going to do something else." And always be aware, there may be occasions where they really do know the answer!
Job Applicants	If you're a hiring manager or recruiter, watch out for the charmer who leaks contempt: she may be more of a problem than an asset to your company. Make sure you check all her references and ask each reference to give you three more people who know the applicant (such as a next-door neighbor, members of a book club, or former coworkers) whom you can talk to—people not listed by the applicant. That's the way the Feds do it, and it works. A little research up front can save you thousands of wasted training dollars and hundreds of hours in rehiring people because no one can work with the new gal!

on how to be prepare your brain and body *before* you need a cold steak for that black eye:

1. **Preawareness:** Just as athletes envision themselves playing a perfect game, you can prepare your brain for any of the potential stressors in your life. To rehearse your reactions, think of several hypothetical dangerous stressors—a carjacking, a robbery, an attempted rape—and imagine what you would do if you were faced with that dangerous situation. "Rehearsing" these next steps, even in your brain, will help you think straight when you are caught off guard.

2. **Awareness:** Be aware of your surroundings at all times. Don't walk with your head down. Criminals say the first thing they look for in potential victims is someone who exhibits nervous behavior. As a good friend of mine, Frank Marsh, who works for the National Drug Intelligence Center cautions, "Once his shoulders are puffed out and his chin is pulled in toward his chest like a bull ready to charge, be forewarned! He might be deciding if he wants to go around you—or through you!"

3. **Stay Calm and Escape:** When confronted with someone who is obviously using the most primitive part of his brain, speak in a calm tone of voice. To stay safe, it's your job to get him back to a balanced state so you can leave unharmed. To create a state of safety, tell the normally rational person who is suddenly out of control, "I don't plan on causing you any harm. I'm leaving. You are safe." And in response to anything he says after that, simply say, "You're right, I'm sorry." (Without sarcasm.) Then leave as soon as possible. ○

Application: Putting Your Best Face Forward

Your face is a significant source of information about your character, behavior, and overall personality. Depending on your facial features, most people will make snap judgments about you when they meet you for the first time, even if you never speak to them. Some people think a woman with thick lips is sexy, while a woman with thin lips is more conscientious. A man with bugged-out eyes is nervous; a man with a high

7-SECOND FIX

Don't Waste Your Time

The Problem: The VP of training of a large Fortune 100 company showed me these images during a discussion of the universal emotions. On the left, you see her three-year-old daughter showing contempt for a photographer who tried to use a silly feather on a stick to get her to laugh. (Notice the side of her face pulled up in the smirk or half-smile of contempt.) On the right, you see her simply smile demurely in response to another photographer's praise and flattery. Though a three-year-old is hardly our biggest threat, her photos help us clearly see the difference between an innocuous social smile and the smirk of someone who was insulted by what you just did or said.

The Fix: If you're not connecting with the person you want to influence and she leaks contempt, the only quick fix is to turn the task over to someone else. There's nothing you can ever do to remedy contempt; it's a conversation ender. If this is a client, you're going to waste hours and hours trying to win the person over. If this is your teen, you just have to be patient and struggle through.

forehead is intelligent. This "attribution theory" may not be fair, and those strangers' assumptions may not be justified, but it is a fact of life we have to live with each day, and with each new encounter.

We've been basing our emotions and decisions on people's facial expressions since we were in the crib. Imagine that your baby pushes against a loose gate at the top of the stairs of a house she has never visited before. How would you respond? Your baby can spot your terror a mile away; she'll recognize the fearful expression on your eyebrows, open mouth and taut jaw, and she'll understand that she should not push on that gate.

That's how we learn about the world—when young infants and children are confronted with an unfamiliar event, they look at their parents' facial expressions for clues on how to respond. In one study, 75 percent of babies whose mothers' faces betrayed no fear crawled out over a "visual cliff"—a glass-covered space that had a relatively frightening deep end—merely on the basis of their mothers' happy and confident smiles. But if a mother's face revealed fear, even its most subtle expression, not one baby would take that risk.

By watching adults' facial expressions and listening to their tone of voice, babies as young as ten months old can use emotional information to decide what to do. This social referencing is something adults do every day—we receive silent feedback from all the people who cross our path hour after hour.

Social referencing is an indispensable skill that helps us throughout our lives; it teaches us how to recognize, understand, and appropriately respond to the angry man who steals our parking spot, our crying coworker two offices down who recently lost her husband, and our deceptive teen who recently started smoking. And it also means that you have to be aware that people are watching *your* face and deciphering *your* expressions all the time.

So what is your face saying to others? Did you know that if, while your face is at rest, your forehead is smooth and wrinkle free and your mouth slightly curved upward, most people will think of you as friendly, likable, sympathetic, considerate, positive, smart, balanced, and good-humored? But if your facial norm is the opposite, where your forehead is wrinkled and your mouth is slightly turned down, people may think that you're aggressive, uptight, distressed, unbalanced, unhappy, you have a short fuse, and you're quick to judge others. Consider this your success wake-up call to make sure your face conveys the same message as your voice and your actions. If you have droopy dog wrinkles, make a concerted effort to hold a social smile on your face, and be sure the rest of your body language is open and inviting. You'll certainly work on that with the exercises at the end of the chapter.

Another way to use your face to convey your message is to combine gestures and expressions into one action: facial fondling.

Facial Fondling

Unless you have an identical twin, no one has a face quite like yours. Your face allows you to communicate with others and to fully enjoy your five senses. It's only natural to want to touch your face. But turn the other cheek and you'll see that some of the signals you're sending could be giving others the wrong impression.

▶ *Face Resting on Hand Versus Hand Resting on Face.* Believe it or not, there is a difference here. If your face is resting on your hand, you appear bored, as it seems like the hand is the only thing keeping your head up. Conversely, resting your hand on your face makes you seem interested and thinking or considering what someone else is saying or doing. So whenever you find yourself resting your face on your hand, switch it around so your hand rests on your face. You will seem interested and contemplative even if, on the inside, you are bored and drowsy. (*Remember:* body language isn't what you *want* it to mean but how it's being perceived!)

▶ *Scratching Your Nose.* Besides helping you to smell things, the nose is a powerful indicator of what's going on in your head. When we deceive others (especially by lying), the blood vessels in the nose can constrict and get red, almost like a blush. People will instinctively draw their hand to their schnozz to cover this up. However, men have erectile tissue in their nose, so they might be scratching it because they are thinking of something . . . else.

Then again, it could just be an itch.

▶ *Hand over Mouth.* Mouth touchers be warned: this classic sign of shock and surprise, especially if the hand covers the entire mouth, has been interpreted by many as a sign of disagreement, as if you're sealing your lips shut.

Fingers to the lips suggest you have a lot on your mind.

Even though we might not say it, a few fingers over the lips are an almost symbolic way of indicating that there is an internal dialogue going on. While some people believe it is a clear signal of disapproval of what is being said or done, others consider it a sign of deep thought. If you find yourself making this gesture, it is in your best interest to quickly move your hand into the next move . . .

▶ *Grasping or Stroking Your Chin, aka the Chin Grab.* The chin grab is considered a sign of thinking and consideration. This signal is often used when world leaders and the elite rest their hands on their faces. Your hand on your chin can send the message to others of wisdom and contemplation, but if you're not careful, it can end up looking like the dreaded Face Resting on Hand move. To see an expert at this gesture, look at computer guru Steve Jobs—in almost every speech he makes, this gesture will pop up. Want to look smarter in a pinch? Do what Steve does and reach for your chin!

▶ *The Blank Face.* We all have a "resting" face where we are not making any expressions. Our facial muscles are relaxed, and we're not smiling, frowning, or making any indication of an emotional signal. It's just . . . blank. Even so, this expression tells people one thing: DO NOT DISTURB. Not sending facial signals one way or another is an instant barrier to others. To many, you will not appear friendly; nor will you appear aggressive. You just might be too much of an enigma.

Always keep an expression on your face, but make sure it's a good one, even if it's something as simple as thinking, "I know something you don't know." When your parents told you that if you kept making that face, it would stick that way, they might have been on to something. A lifetime of scowling, grumpiness, and grimaces will leave its mark. Better start smiling, stat! Start with these exercises to help you put your best face forward.

My super-friendly uncle Francie was always a bit hard to read because of his blank expression.

Day 6: Best Face Forward

These exercises will help you sharpen your accuracy, so you can spot and detect the Dangerous Four before any trouble arises. They'll also help you create a more pleasant and welcoming resting face.

▶ *Take Me Out to the Ball Game.* Visit Six Flags today or go to a hockey game or a high school football game tonight. Go to any large group environment, where you'll see the gamut of emotions, and simply practice the art of observation.

▶ *Make a Face.* Take a mirror and make the different facial expressions seen in the photos in this chapter. Then, to see what your face is saying to others complete the following facial experiment:

Step 1. Have a friend take three photos of your face:

1. **At Rest:** What your face would look like if you were sitting in your home or office relaxed. Think about nothing, as if you were in a quiet daze.
2. **Slightly Smiling:** Only smile a splash with your mouth, but do not wrinkle your forehead. Think to yourself that something exciting is about to happen to you.
3. **Slightly Stressed/Angry:** Subtle wrinkles in the forehead, mouth taut—serious. Think to yourself that you are about to receive a call in which your friend is going to tell you that people in the office are spreading gossip about you.

Step 2. Attach each photo to a piece of paper and below the photo list the following attributes (please circle one answer, A or B, for each of the following):

A	B
Happy	Unhappy
Friendly	Aggressive
Sympathetic	Uptight
Positive	Negative

Smart	Overcompensates for weaknesses
Balanced	Unbalanced
Good sense of humor	Short fuse
Other: _____	Other: _____

Step 3. Next have your friends or family members go out in public and ask ten people to review one photo each. Ask them to circle either A or B in each of the line items above. They should pick the word that they think best describes the person in the photo. So your friends will need to get thirty people total to rank the photos. Have your friends tell the participants that they are testing *their* ability to read others' subtle facial expressions. This way the participants won't feel like they are hurting anyone's feelings if they check a negative answer.

Step 4. Check out the results; see if your face really does say more than you think. Are you surprised at the characteristics people checked for your baseline photo? Does your baseline photo have more in common with your subtle happy photo or your subtle stressed photo? How can this information help you use the New Body Language to get what you want in life?

▶ *Play Charades, Pictionary, or Other Nonverbal Board Games.* You can't go wrong testing your newfound body language and facial expression knowledge by playing a game. Invite some friends over and simply have fun. If you haven't told them that you're doing the 7-Day Program yet, wait! What you've already learned will help you study the nonverbal interactions between team players when they win, lose, or are simply thinking to themselves.

▶ *Take Your Emotions to New Heights.* My good friend Chris Ulrich (a member of my second Body Language Power Team) is an improvisational (improv) genius. He showed me this exercise, which he learned while taking an improv class in Chicago. It's used by actors and comedians to increase their abilities to convey a message with word choices, tone of voice, body language, and facial expression, which ultimately give them greater range and emotional diversity. Even if you don't do improv, stand-up, or acting, if you follow the five steps below, you'll gain insight into how you manifest your emotions physically.

Step 1. Pick an emotion to use during the exercise (anything will do): happiness, sadness, anger, disgust, jealousy, guilt, surprise, fear, anxiety, and so on. (You can also randomly pull the emotion out of a hat or bag.)

Step 2. Get a partner, face each other, and stand at least twenty feet away from one another.

Step 3. Explain to your partner that you are both going to experience and demonstrate the selected emotion in the subtlest form, which we'll call a Level One. Then take a step closer to one another, and express that emotion as a Level Two, until you eventually reach Level Ten, which is the most intense version of that emotion and you're right in each other's faces. (Be sure to start subtly so you actually have somewhere to go when you get to the most intense level.)

Step 4. Then back up, step-by-step, softening the emotion until you are back at Level One. (You can repeat this exercise with a different emotion as often as you like.)

Step 5. Review what happened by answering the following questions:

- Did one of you max out on your emotions before Level Ten? (This exercise is especially helpful to people whose emotions tend to go from Level One or Two to Level Ten, without realizing how quickly they escalate. These are the people who push others away with their intense anger, or have their feelings slightly hurt at Level One and jump immediately to Level Ten, devastated and ready for revenge!)
- If you maxed out your emotions before Level Ten, how can that information help *you* deal with your emotions in real-life situations? (People sometimes find that simply practicing the midrange emotional response gives them a better perspective on healthy, alternative responses.)

▶ *Breathe in Calm, Breathe out Fear.* While with ATF, I was certified as an Escape and Evade instructor, a self-defense course whose main objective was for us to escape safely. It was like a college course for fighting. The curriculum included striking and kicking all the major nerve points, standing and kneeling combat scenarios, and even disarming a suspect with a gun who we thought was going to kill us (a skill none of us hoped we'd ever have to use). One of the most valuable skills I learned in the course can help you when fear explodes without warning.

During fearful situations, we all go through a certain cascade of biological reactions. Our hearts begin to beat faster, and we have very little time to think about what to do before our fine motor skills begin to falter (such as writing, drawing, holding small objects, or buttoning a shirt) and our ability to function begins to decline. Before our complex motor skills disappear (such as large muscle movements in the arms and legs), our blood pressure shoots through the roof, and our rational thinking shuts down. What a picnic, huh?

To short-circuit this fear-based "gray-out," you can implement a valuable breathing technique called *tactical breathing* that cops use in combat. This easy-to-learn breathing procedure instantly clears your muddled mind and can give you optimum physical and mental control within seconds. Try it for one full cycle right now, with closed eyes, if you'd like:

Step 1. Breathe in through the nose for a count of four, filling your lower belly.

Step 2. Hold your breath for a count of four.

Step 3. Exhale through your lips like a whistle for a count of four.

Step 4. Hold your breath for a count of four and then repeat the cycle.

Step 5. Repeat for four sets.

Don't let fear stop you from taking action in your life! Fear is only as powerful as its representation in your mind. By using tactical breathing in high-anxiety situations, you can alter the intensity of your fear, which will give you the courage and willingness to go out and do something new. Go ahead, give yourself permission to break out of your comfort zone and grow.

EIGHT

Day 7: The QWQ Formula and Other Advanced Techniques

The optimist sees opportunity in every danger; the pessimist sees danger in every opportunity.
—WINSTON CHURCHILL (1874-1965), FORMER BRITISH PRIME MINISTER

M ost of us talk way too much. Our culture tends to mistakenly honor "talkers" as people who have influence—but you can get much more useful information by asking powerful questions and then sitting back and waiting to hear the answers.

I recently heard about Cindy, the mother of one of my employees, a seventh-grade teacher who used the QWQ—Question, Wait, Question—formula (which I'll describe in a moment) to discourage the destructive practice of "slam" books in her classroom. If you don't know what a slam book is, it is a notebook junior high school girls pass around that contains hurtful gossip used to taunt and bully their peers and sometimes even teachers. The person who keeps the book starts by asking a question such as, "What do you think of Georgia stealing Beth's boyfriend?" or "How can we get Mike to break up with Kara?" The book is then passed around for each contributor to fill in her response.

Many teachers struggle to confiscate these books, but the girls who create them deny their existence. Cindy had previously warned students that slam books would yield poor conduct grades, talks with parents,

Name: Jesse Swart
Age: 32
Occupation: Systems Analyst

What was holding you back? My background is deeply "technical": top science schools (MIT) and high-tech jobs since high school, replete with the stereotypical nerd environments. I have felt like, in my communication with other people, there's often an important part of the puzzle missing. Some have told me I act arrogant, and others have said I "lack confidence." Usually, after talking with someone for a few moments, I think I come across as insecure, but I'm not sure what I'm doing to send that message. I wanted to be seen as more confident, primarily in dating, although also at work and social settings. I also wanted to work on any quirks or other negative things I might be doing that keep me from being "charming" in general. And I certainly wanted to avoid appearing "arrogant."

I'd tried to address this issue on my own—I've asked friends for feedback, read a few articles and books. I even took a sales-related job to spend more time working with people. But I had trouble finding good feedback on what I am doing and suggestions on what to try next.

How have you changed? After Janine's BLPT training, I noticed an improvement with just one technique—standing with feet wider apart. With the first few of her suggestions and the team's help, I've made more significant changes. Family and friends have all noticed a difference since I implemented those first deceptively simple changes in my posture, all the way up to the surprising secret: attitude. But it's also been very helpful to learn how to ask powerful questions.

I've always asked lots of questions. I guess having a background with computers, I got used to issuing commands. Computers don't care what you ask, even if you ask the same thing over and over. I'd also made a habit of asking questions to which I already knew the answer. Even though people communicate so much in *how* they answer, they are not computers and they don't like being interrogated.

The biggest change I've made was how to ask about a particularly telling body language movement. Janine had us practice the question, "Maybe I'm wrong here, but in the last moment or so it seems like there's more to this story." This gives the other person room to reveal more of what's on his or her mind without being forced into a game of twenty questions.

Perhaps the most powerful thing I learned from Janine was about the word *try*. During one of the days' exercises, she caught me saying, "I'll try to act more like that." Very Yoda-like, Janine told me to drop *try*. Somewhere in the back of my mind, I must have known that it would make a world of a difference to stop using, *I'll try* or *I think I can*. So, instead, I said, "I *will* use a more steady, deliberate, measured, relaxed pace in my movements, walking, and speaking." Until I had removed *I'll try*, I hadn't noticed just how uncertain and tentative I sounded. So I said it again. And that time I believed it.

referrals to the principal—but nothing seemed to stop the problem. The QWQ formula finally helped her win.

One afternoon, Cindy noticed what appeared to be a slam book being passed around. After class Cindy confronted the suspected keeper of the book. The girl thought she was slick and handed over a dummy spiral notebook. With one look, Cindy knew this wasn't the true slam book—so she mentally pulled out the QWQ formula.

Looking directly at the girl, Cindy asked, "Is there any reason why you wouldn't give me the real book?"

The student protested, swearing that was the only book, giving the typical teenage girl attitude. Cindy tilted her head and said somewhat sarcastically, "Really?"

The girl continued to protest about how that was the only book, why would she give a fake book, that she was being wrongly accused. Cindy just **W.A.I.T.**ed (Why Am I Talking?).

The teenage girl continued to talk, and talk, and talk. Cindy didn't say a word and just let the girl keep talking. Finally, she asked the girl, "Is there anything you would like to get off your chest?"

The girl reached into her bag and handed over another book—the real slam book. Cindy was amazed at how quickly her newfound questioning technique led to the truth and resolved the situation with less time and less drama.

Accuracy: Ask Powerful Questions

Listening is a critical skill many of us overlook. After all, we are fascinating people and we want to share that! Luckily, as experts on ourselves, we have tons of information to share with everyone else.

I'm kidding, of course—but this wealth of personal information is precisely *why* you should listen instead of speak. Powerful people recognize that sharing too much personal information can weaken them, so they encourage others to speak instead. Just think of the power and control you have when you listen rather than speak: they divulge their thoughts, you filter the information, you ask more questions, you get more information. You get to direct the conversation with your questions, and you learn more detail about what matters to you.

Powerful people also realize that most people love to talk about themselves. Listeners are considered "great conversationalists." You would be surprised how many people, after talking to an active listener for a few hours, come away thinking they had a great conversation, when *they* did almost all of the talking.

Perhaps most important, when you actively listen to people's personal stories, you enhance their feelings of safety and trust. In any situation, listening builds rapport.

When you were younger, someone may have said to you, "We have two eyes, two ears, and one mouth—keep them in proportion." That's great advice for us all. Perhaps an even better expression comes from my mentor J. J. Newberry, who says, "The person who controls the questions controls the conversation."

Powerful questions are those that are crafted to elicit the most useful information in the least amount of time. By asking powerful questions you'll be able to ·

- Direct conversations and keep the conversation moving forward.
- Gather information and insights about others.
- Assess and clarify problems or issues and aid in understanding.
- Show respect for others' opinions.
- Facilitate action or change.
- Unlock awareness in others.
- Evaluate people's progress toward their personal and professional goals.

Following are some of my favorite powerful questions. As you'll notice, I favor using "How" and "What" questions:

"How" Questions

How do you like [your job, your new house, being a parent, etc.]?
How was your weekend?
How's your week going?
How did that come about?
How did you think/feel/act?
How did you react?
How did you cope in the past?

"What" Questions

What happened?
What part did you play in it?
What did you think about that?
What makes you think that?
What did that mean to you?
What did you mean by that? Would you give me an example?
What might you do differently next time?
What did you learn from it?

"Where" Questions

Where do you see yourself . . . ?
Where will that get you?
Where can we start to make a change?
Where did it go wrong?
Where did it go right?

Why You Should Avoid "Why" Questions

"Why" questions are not useful to establish rapport, as they often make people defensive, but they are great when someone is lying to you. "When" questions are too close-ended and do not help get people talking.

During the rapport-building phase of any conversation, avoid using "why" questions. When you challenge people to answer why something is or was one way or another, they tend to get defensive. We all have a strong emotional connection to our beliefs of why something happened. Trigger that connection and you shut down the thinking process, and often your rapport. You're much better off using "what" or "how" over "why" questions.

For example, instead of asking, "Why are we here today?" you could say, "What's on the agenda for today?" The second question will get you the answer you're looking for while being less judgmental than the first. Think about the difference: "Why did you put Steve in charge of the project?" versus "How does putting Steve in charge of the project help you?"

How to Use the Questions

The questions themselves are most effective if you learn when to ask them. Remember when we baselined Woody Allen in Chapter 2? Let's say you were observing Allen and, suddenly, he changed from his norm of being closed off and nervous to more open. Maybe he took his hands out of his pockets and left them hanging at his sides while he stood straight and tall. (Maybe he even stood like Sarah Jessica Parker in the Superman pose.) Noting the difference, you might wonder, "Hmm, why is he more comfortable all of a sudden? Does he trust me? Or is he just *trying* to convince me that he's more comfortable?"

Rather than attempting to mind-read, you're better off just asking him. Sound ridiculous? Actually, asking your target why he feels uncomfortable is just about the fastest way to uncover the truth that you can imagine. A Powerful Question can create discomfort, but an All-Powerful Question allows you to just come right out and ask what's wrong. And very often, the person will tell you.

You can either wait for a Probing Point to arise naturally in the conversation, or you can create one with a Powerful Question by raising an issue or topic that's likely to make your target slightly uncomfortable. These are fun—you're deliberately changing the chemistry of the encounter in order to gather useful information. (As you can imagine, we used this technique all the time in ATF.) The resulting deviation from their norm will give you the opening—then you can move in for the kill with the All-Powerful Question.

You saw a version of the following chart in Chapter 2. Now you're going to take it to the next level with Powerful Questions.

Situation	Norm	Powerful Question	Probing Point	All-Powerful Question
Flirting	60% eye contact	"So, are you married?"	More or less eye contact	"Maybe I'm wrong, Lorraine, but it seems like you're a little nervous."
Job Interview	Relaxed and open body language	"What would your last boss say about your weaknesses?"	Crosses arms and legs, creating a barrier	"It sounds like you are uncomfortable talking about..."

Continued

Situation	Norm	Powerful Question	Probing Point	All-Powerful Question
Business Negotiation	Leaning back while steepling	"How did you arrive at that price?"	Leans forward and uses the honest and sincere open-palm gesture	"Really, Caileen?" (said with a confused tone). Then say NOTHING until she explains it all again!
Buying a Car	Hands on hips with feet >10" apart	"How much more will the car cost if I add an extended warranty?"	Hands go into pockets (with thumbs hidden) and stance widens	Tilt your head, and say NOTHING until he adds additional information. Then say, "Tell me more about that, Leif."
Confronting Someone	Facing you, with his arms relaxed down by his side	"Did you drink my last beer?"	He still remains facing you with his face, but his belly button turns to the door	"David, is there something you'd like to get off your chest?"
Making a Request	Relaxed facial expression	"How would you like to be the lead on this project?"	Her nose does a quick wrinkle and when she says, "Not a problem, I'll do a great job for you," she makes a shoulder shrug.	"Maybe I'm wrong, Kerry, but it seems to me that you are uncertain about something." After Kerry answers, next ask, "Is there any reason why this project might not get done?"

7-SECOND FIX

From Powerless to Powerful

The Problem: When the conversation gets deep, people can take refuge in self-touch gestures, like the one pictured on the left. When you see a person make this gesture during questioning, it could be a defensive maneuver against an overly invasive question—or you may have hit a Probing Point.

The Fix: If you notice yourself in this critical pose, simply shift your hand slightly up to your chin—you'll look more thoughtful than nervous.

Application: Confront and Control with Compassion

When I started working for ATF in the early winter of 1992, I trained with many different investigators. The bureau wanted newbies like me to see different inspection styles and adapt what we liked to make it our own. The investigator I learned the most from was a man we'll call "Don."

Don taught me what *not* to do.

One Friday, Don and I visited the small gun shop of an eighty-year-old dealer. The old man sold no more than ten guns per month, and ATF had not been by in years. Even though he was supposed to complete paperwork within twenty-four hours of a sale, the old man's wife did it weekly.

While this was a violation of the Federal Firearms Regulations, let's just say it wasn't like the guy was selling AK-47s to gangbangers. Don, who had the authority to be flexible on how the problem could be resolved, chose to use intimidating body language and dominating, condescending voice tones instead. "We'll be back next week, and you'd better have your paperwork updated when we get here!" he boomed.

"No problem," the old man respectfully replied. "We'll do it over the weekend."

Don glared. "WE won't do anything over the weekend! YOU will do it over the weekend!"

I was stunned. It was a mere filing violation, for crying out loud. I would not be surprised if the old man never trusted anyone from the government again.

Don showed me why the most successful interviewers and investigators don't use good cop/bad cop anymore. That approach simply doesn't work—because if you don't have a baseline, you'll never know what's causing the suspect's anxiety. Is it because you're screaming in his face or because he's lying? When you confront someone with angry tones, all you do is make her freeze or flee—and neither one gets you what you need.

What has your confrontational baseline been up until now? During conflicts with others, do you stop and ask yourself what might be causing a person to act this way? Remember that you are a representative of your company, family, or group of friends. If a person were to judge them by your behavior, would that raise or lower the value of that group?

Don must have missed this valuable life lesson. But this experience made it crystal clear to me: you can ask powerful questions and give powerful commands to get people to do things without giving up likability or respect. Two powerful techniques—the QWQ formula and anchoring—will take you miles beyond what bullies like Don could ever achieve.

The QWQ Formulas

You've learned about Probing Points, Powerful Questions, and All-Powerful Questions. These three components make up the three-step method that hostage negotiators, schoolteachers, the most effective parents, and people just like you can use to find out the truth. The basic QWQ formula goes like this:

1. **Q:** Ask a Powerful Question to search for a Probing Point.
2. **W:** Is short for **W.A.I.T:** "Why Am I Talking?" an acronym I learned from Wanda Pease, an HR executive with a lot of experience in interviewing. It means to wait and listen, truly listen, to what the other person has to say. W.A.I.T. until the other person says *everything* he or she has to say. (Silence, listening, and asking Powerful Questions are the most powerful tools any hostage negotiator has, and the same is true for you.)
3. **Q:** Ask another Powerful Question or an All-Powerful Question.

Different QWQ formulas can be used in any situation in which you want to ferret out more information—whether you're negotiating a better price for a car or trying to find out if your daughter is lying to you, this process will get you there. You can even further refine the process, depending on the situation. Check out a few of my special "formulas" for finding the truth.

▶ *Formula One—Questioning to assign the person a positive trait.* It doesn't matter if you are speaking with a barricaded person, an interviewee, or a date, remember that the person in front of you has pride. Rather than being negative and saying, "Don't lie to me," suggest the quality you *want* to see. As my friend James Cavanaugh, ATF Special Agent in Charge always says, "Credit people with the quality you want them to produce and normally they'll accept it, even feel bound to it."

1. **Question 1: Assign the trait:** "You're a trustworthy person, right?"
2. **W.A.I.T.** The person will respond, "Yes."

3. **Question 2: Validate that claim:** "I know you are. And if you said you were going to do something, you'd do it, right?"

4. **W.A.I.T.** Again, the person will most likely say, "Yes."

5. **Question 3: Compare yourself to the person:** "I know you are the kind of person who keeps her word." Then add, "I'm like that, too. If I say I'm going to do it, I'm going to do it."

This formula sets the stage for future interactions, so the person will follow through. You get people to state who they are or who they think they are; then you'll work with that instilled trait to achieve the next level. After all, you want others to feel good, not bad. Who are you more likely to be receptive to—someone who recognizes your positive characteristics, or someone who belittles you by detailing each flaw?

Here are some examples of other ways to assign someone a positive trait that you want them to have:

- **To Your Employee:** "Look, Joe, you're a good employee. Look at the sales you've closed over the year. You work hard, right?"
- **To Your Spouse:** "Honey, aren't you thoughtful? Even when it's difficult, you always put us first, right?"
- **To Your New Date Mate:** "You treat women well, right? I thought so. I can tell that you're the kind of guy who's respectful and you keep your word. I'm just like that; if I tell you I'll be there at 7:00 P.M., I'll be there at 7:00."
- **To Your Toddler or Teen:** "Angus, you're a good listener, right? And you're a good boy, right? I know you are, honey. I'm just like you; when you want me to listen, I listen."

▶ *Formula Two—Information gathering in less confrontational negotiations.* You can use this formula when you notice the person's normal behavior change and you see several Probing Points. You sense the person may be experiencing an emotion that conflicts with what he or she is saying.

1. **Question 1: "Maybe I'm wrong here, but it seems to me that you are . . ."** For example, happy about losing your job, upset about

going out with her again, angry that we are going to my mother's for Christmas.

2. **W.A.I.T.**

Note: If the person doesn't share with you his or her real concerns and still seems to be holding something back, continue with the following questions:

3. **Question 2: "[Say the person's name], what's *REALLY* going on?"**
4. **W.A.I.T.**
5. **Question 3: "Tell me more about that."**
6. **W.A.I.T.**

This formula will help a person open up really quickly. You'll be amazed at how fast people will tell you extremely deep and personal feelings.

▶ *Formula Three—Detecting deception and forcing the deceiver to confess.* You don't have to be an ATF special agent to require the use of this formula. This technique works in countless situations.

1. **Question 1: "[Said in a nonaccusatory tone] Is there any reason why . . .?"** "Is there any reason why you told me that you were out with Michael, but two people told me they saw you holding hands with a woman?" "Is there any reason why the TV is on a channel that you are not allowed to watch?" "Is there any reason why you're nervous about making this merger?" "Is there any reason why you would leave something off your résumé?"
2. **W.A.I.T.**
3. **Question 2: "Really?"**
4. **W.A.I.T.** (Remain quiet until he speaks again. *Whoever speaks next, loses.* Truthful people are okay with silence, but liars need to be believed, so when you look at the person you are confronting, tilt your head to the side and say nothing and see what happens. DO NOT SPEAK UNTIL HE TELLS HIS STORY AGAIN.)
5. **Question 3: "[Say the person's name], is there something you want to get off your chest?"**
6. **W.A.I.T.**

Now, if this technique can work for law enforcement, and a frustrated seventh-grade teacher, imagine what it can do for you! Trust me: the results will amaze you.

Anchoring

You know how when your doctor taps that little hammer just below your knee, your leg jerks forward? Or when someone unexpectedly squirts you in the face with a water pistol, you flinch and blink, right? These reflexes are built in, innate. You don't need to learn them—you have them from birth.

Then there's the other kind of reflex, the bell-ringing-dog-salivating Pavlovian response reflex. We learned about that in Psych 101: Russian scientist Ivan Petrovich Pavlov sounded a bell when a dog was fed, and later the dog would salivate merely at the sound of the bell, with or without the food. Pavlov proved to the world that environmental events that previously had no relation to a reflex could, through experience, trigger that reflex. We get these "conditioned reflexes" when, through exposure to some combination of experiences, we unconsciously connect that event or stimulus to the reflex.

We have thousands of these conditioned reflexes, or anchors, in our lives. For instance, when I hear Madonna's 1980s hit song "Crazy for You," I'm immediately transported back to the junior high school dance when Peter B. gave me my first real kiss on the dance floor. When I smell coffee (and I hate the smell of coffee), I think of being a teenager, filling donuts with jelly at 5:00 A.M. at Mister Donuts on Lexington Street in Waltham, Massachusetts. If I see an empty Dunkin' Donuts coffee cup, I think of my dad, my sister Caileen, and my deceased uncle Francie, because they all love Dunkin' Donuts coffee. All of these anchors involve a stimulus (the song, the smell of coffee, the sight of the cup) that conditions our mind, heart, and emotions to respond a certain way (the thrill of that first kiss, the fatigue of working at 5:00 A.M., the love I have for my family).

We talked about anchoring others briefly in Chapter 6 when we talked about handshakes. When you consciously anchor someone, every time you touch that person (or they hear that sound or feel that movement) in the same way, you can retrigger that anchor to evoke that same feeling or image.

Anchoring can be done to others to put them in a state of mind that you desire, or you can do it to yourself to change your mood or feelings. Let's explore how to anchor someone else first.

1. Establish an Anchor. You can establish a physical and vocal anchor when you meet someone. When shaking hands, say something positive such as, "I am so glad to finally meet you. I've heard such good things about you." Then take it a step further and when you sit down, touch her lower arm and compliment her on something, "I love your name." Then close with why you like what you liked about the thing you complimented. For instance, when I interviewed my intern, I said, "I love your name, Jerusalem. It's so unique, it will be easy for me to remember; it stands out, it pops!" Other ways to create a positive anchor include smiling as you lean forward slightly while relaxing your posture, nodding your head, and using subvocal expressions such as "uh-huh" or "um-hmmm."

Think of a stimulus (a touch or a word) that you can attach to the most emotional moment of your interaction (such as an enthusiastic first meeting). Pick a stimulus not usually triggered, such as touch to the forearm or shoulder, or an unusual sound ("it pops!")—this is the anchor. Install the anchor as early as possible in your relationship, such as immediately upon meeting someone, with your simultaneous handshake/forearm touch, "I like your name, it pops!"

2. Repeat Placement of the Anchor. Use the anchor again in a similar situation so that anchor will be conditioned to that state. For example, touch the person on the arm in the same exact place, with the same amount of pressure, when you hear something you like during your discussion at the meeting. On Jerusalem's first day on the job, to eliminate first-day jitters and build rapport, I asked her an open-ended question: "What's the story behind your name?" When Jerusalem responded with, "Put it this way: I have a sister and her name is [pause] Bethlehem," I burst out laughing and anchored that same touch again.

Not only did I connect my touch with my enthusiasm at meeting her, I also solidified the anchor with positive feelings about her family, history, religion, and culture.

3. Activate the Anchor. Activate the anchor so you will get the result you want right away. For example, when I want Jerusalem to put her heart into a project, I'll activate that same anchor and pair it with, "I know you'll do a great job on this." Activating the anchor when I ask her to do a task creates the feeling of added support, that we all—her family, her beliefs, everything she holds dear—believe in her ability to get the job done.

You can also create a negative anchor by changing your vocal qualities to clash with the other person's tone, pitch, and rate of speech. (Anything you do to deliberately break rapport might create a negative anchor.) A negative anchor is useful when someone is holding something back from you or she is lying, because, ultimately, we all want to be in rapport with one another. The negative anchor gives people a subtle, uncomfortable push to lay all the cards on the table. Once they do come clean, be sure to instill or go back to a previous positive anchor that you created for them.

DITCH THE HEAVY ANCHOR

Did you ever wonder why actors in Hollywood who finally get their big break and start rolling in the big bucks often leave the person who supported them up the challenging ladder of success? Well, their former spouses might have been with them during the tough times and have now become an anchor for struggle and pain. Their new love interests knows them for who they are now—superstars! Prevent this from happening in your relationship by constantly updating your positive experiences with significant others, so they have some strong and positive anchors in their memory bank.

▶ *Anchoring Yourself.* While I was pregnant, every time I took a bath I listened to Diana Krall music, put lavender essential oil in the tub, and repeated over and over in my head, "peace and serenity." When I had an unexpected C-section some months later, I just thought of the words while lying there in the surgical room, and I was relaxed. And today, whenever I smell lavender or hear a Diana Krall song, I'm immediately transported back to the day I became a new mother and held my newborn son, Angus, the greatest gift of my life.

Other anchors you could use include: imagining a comforting hand on your shoulder; eating a Tic-Tac; wearing a certain perfume or scented lotion; listening to a certain song; looking at a picture; or even squeezing your toes in your shoes.

Anchors can really help us perform at our peak: researchers at the University of Liverpool found that students who wore the same scent (orange or lavender) during studying improved their recall by 15–20 percent. Use the following steps to create your own anchors.

Step 1. Establish an Anchor: Select a feeling or emotion that you would like to have in a particular situation. For instance, you might want to feel happiness and strength when you attend your children's school play, but you know your ex (and the woman he cheated on you with and left you for) will be there.

Step 2. Repeat Placement of the Anchor: Take a minute to recall a time when you felt happy and strong in a big way. If you don't have a personal experience feeling that way, imagine what it would be like to feel this way right now.

Step 3. Visualize the Anchor: Now close your eyes and put yourself there. Remember that day or that place where you felt that powerful way in vibrant intense detail. Like watching a movie on your DVD player, turn up the color, bring the image closer, and make the sounds more audible. Now, choose one or two words to describe that experience, and curl up your toes while you are at the peak of that powerful emotion. And keep them curled.

Step 4. Release and Repeat the Anchor: Let that feeling of strength and happiness crash over you like a wave at the beach on a hot day. It's refreshing. Powerful. It's a new beginning. Now relax your toes, open your eyes, and release that memory. Choose another memory of having that same feeling or emotion, repeat the previous steps, and use the same gesture. Then repeat the entire exercise one more time with a third example.

Step 5. Activate the Anchor: Activate the anchor, scrunch up your toes, and put your new anchor to the test! If your emotion, posture, stance, self-talk, breathing rate, head position, and tone of voice have not changed to that more powerful state, do the process again, but brighten each step with even more color and intensity. Then repeat each step.

Just like Powerful Questions, anchors can have tremendous influence—they can put us in a good mood or a bad mood. They can inspire us to stand up tall and take action, or to get small and not get involved. These two tools are among the most efficient and effective tools in your New Body Language kit.

Day 7: Learn How to Ask Powerful Questions

These specific methods take lots of practice to master—but once you have them down, they are truly the keys to the kingdom. You'll discover far more, and far more quickly, than you ever could before. Use the following exercises to develop these advanced skills.

▶ *Get Personal with Each QWQ Formula.* Your primary exercise for today will be to get familiar with each of the different QWQ formulas.

Formula One: Questioning to assign a positive trait
Formula Two: Information gathering in less confrontational negotiations
Formula Three: Detecting deception and forcing the deceiver to confess

Write down the names of seven different people in your life (one name at the top, per page) in your journal. Next, mentally divide the paper in thirds and write the name of each of the QWQ formulas in each of the sections. Now write an example for each of the formulas that you can use either immediately or some time in the future with the person named at the top of the page. Repeat the process for all seven people and seven pages. This exercise will help train your brain on what to use when.

▶ *Become a QWQ Security Guard.* This afternoon or this evening, visit your local shopping mall, Target, Wal-Mart, or grocery store, and pay attention to how people confront other people at customer service or in the aisles with their kids. Think like an undercover security guard. But instead of watching for items slipped in bags or under shirts, you're listening with your ears, then with your eyes.

What kinds of questions or accusations are people making to one another (who is the persecutor and who's the victim)? How is this working for them? What results are they getting? How do the people on the other end of a poor question or accusation respond verbally and non-verbally? Do they yell, swear, or have a temper tantrum? Does their body language get big or small? Do they bring out any of the power gestures or leak nervousness? Observe seven different people and document the situation in your success journal.

Then after writing a couple of paragraphs about what happened, write your analysis and write the name of the QWQ formula that you would have used in each of the situations. And what exactly would you have said? (You can peek back at the formulas for some additional insight if you need to.)

▶ *Assign Traits to Others.* Are you frustrated with someone in your life? Assign him or her the trait you want the person to have. For instance, this morning my son was playing with an elaborate pop-up book while I was on the phone with one of my sisters. At first I said, "Angus, please put the book back, I'll read it to you when I get off the phone." He ignored me and continued to play with the book. Then I tried QWQ: "Angus, you're a good listener, right?"

He smiled and said, "Yes."

"Do you think you're the best listener in the whole world?" I asked.

He laughed and responded, "YES!"

Then I added, "I know you're the best listener in the whole world; that's one of the many things I love about you. When I ask you to do something, you do it faster than any other kid I know." He smiled. Then I said, "Angus, please put the book back and I'll play with you when I'm done." And he put the book back and began playing with a toy dinosaur instead.

NINE

All Together, Now:
A New Attitude

If you change the way you look at things, the things you look at change.
—Dr. Wayne Dyer (1940–), motivational author

In 2005, when my son, Angus, was born, my husband and I were devastated to find out that his heart was slightly underdeveloped. The doctors said that Angus's heart would take care of itself by the time he turned eight months old. But after my maternity leave ran out four months later, there had been no change in Angus's heart condition. My first day back at the office, I asked my supervisor if I could participate in a work-from-home program for four months until Angus would have his next visit with the cardiologist. I wanted to be nearby in case something unexpected happened to him. Despite the situation, my boss refused, casually saying, "If I let you, everyone else will want to work from home." This response was just the first of dozens of equally cold, dismissive, heartless dismissals that I received at her hand. It sent me on a downward spiral. I felt full of hatred for my boss and the agency. And I fell into a depression.

Each day, I would walk into my office, shut the door, cry, and then send an e-mail to my boss's boss begging to work from home, sometimes even noting my supervisor's on-the-job indiscretions. I was in self-destruct mode and primed to go off, until one day, my former boss, Special Agent Theresa Stoop, knocked on my door. Theresa had just been appointed to be the assistant deputy director of ATF's Training and Professional Development. She now held seniority over my boss's boss, and she had heard of the trouble I was getting myself into.

Name: PK Ewing

Age: 39

Occupation: Professional actor, professional military officer, diplomat, competitive athlete

What was holding you back? For much of my life, my body language was overpowering or too aggressive. Others would say I appeared angry when I was merely concentrating on what they were saying. My body language was out of sync with my intentions, but I did not know how to change it.

How have you changed? After my makeover, I learned that being congruent in appearance and spoken word makes your communication very powerful. People "hear and see" you better; they aren't distracted by what you are *showing* and missing what you are *saying*.

I've been a Marine officer for over sixteen years. I know how to command, how to deliver a commanding presence, and inspire others to action. Adding the knowledge I learned from Janine made communicating that presence easier and more fluid. I've used this knowledge to become more approachable and appear less intense.

Make no mistake, since the 7-Day Makeover, the trajectory of my life changed drastically: I found the strength to leave a destructive and all-consuming relationship. I embarked on developing a speaking career of my own. I reconnected with old friends and became very close to my fellow makeover team members. My social life and my relationships with my friends improved. I've been able to avoid misunderstandings and defuse tensions more easily. I enjoy the whole process of communicating with others and connecting in a way I did not before Janine's course. I've even begun hosting a weekly radio show.

My advice to anyone reading this book is: do the work. The magic lies in the process. Do the exercises and incorporate them into your life slowly to ensure that they become habit. That way change will take hold and everything will improve.

The program changed my life because it reminded me of something I had let slip from my consciousness: attitude and confidence are key. My naval academy class motto is "Fortune Favors the Bold." To be bold, you must have self-confidence and attitude. What most will not realize is the fact that your attitude carries your body language. Body language cannot be faked. Your attitude colors it and gives it animation. When your attitude is right, your body language is right—and vice versa.

She said very little to me that day; she simply listened, and listened, and listened. When I was done talking, crying, and being sarcastic, she opened her arms up and stretched them out toward me, as if she were about to scoop a younger toddler, and said, "Janine, you have enough to worry about at home. Give this problem over to me. I will take it from here." That one simple gesture of opening her arms gave me a lump in my throat and I cried again, but this time, tears of hope ran down my cheeks. I finally felt understood, listened to, and safe.

Scientists estimate that approximately 40 percent of our happiness comes from our genes. Ten percent comes from our life's circumstances (getting a raise, losing weight, buying a new car or house, having another baby). The remaining 50 percent of our happiness comes from doing for others. But you don't have to be Mother Teresa to get that "helper's high." You can get it every day, simply by making the decision to treat others with respect, to make a genuine commitment to understand their needs, and to try to help them fulfill those needs while you fulfill your own. Once you can achieve that kind of genuine caring—in which you watch, listen, learn, and respond with compassion—you'll have moved to the third level of the New Body Language: attitude.

In this chapter, you'll take everything you learned in the previous seven days and put it together to help you get whatever you need and truly want in life. First, we'll look at a few global strategies to help you continue to smoothly move toward a winning attitude. You'll learn how to quash negative internal chatter and use easy tools to change perspective.

You'll change the focus from what *you* want to what *others* want—because when you help them get what they want, a window to endless abundance will open for *you*. As Stephen Covey once said, "Seek first to understand, then to be understood."

7-Second Fix

Love Isn't Blind

The Problem: In the photo on the left, you'll see that the man has his right arm behind his blind date, his belly button facing toward her, and his right leg up on the couch showing way too much of his bits. Not only is the woman giving him the cold shoulder with her belly button all covered up, but she's also creating a wall with her arms, her naughty bits are deep undercover, her feet are angled away from him, and she's so uncomfortable she's grabbing two of her right fingers with her left hand.

The Fix: You like her, but she's closed up. So create balance with your body. For instance, if you have an arm in her territory, balance it out with the opposite leg in an open figure four leg cross. You'll appear less aggressive and more confident.

The Third "A": Attitude

When it comes to using the New Body Language to get what you want, it's important to understand that *having* a good attitude and *showing* a good attitude are two different things. One person could be really positive about his life, but not be cheerful or full of life. He may be perceived as having a bad attitude. Another person may be perceived as having a good attitude because she smiles and has a peppy tone of voice. In reality, the person with the smile may complain a lot and only work hard when others are around.

Sam Glenn, author of the book *A Kick in the Attitude,* calls attitude our "personal trademark." What has your trademark been lately? Powerful, confident, happy? Insecure, angry, depressing? Fearful and anxious? Unstoppable? When you begin to choose the attitude that both fits your intention and the situation at hand, your health will get better, your relationships will be fuller, conflicts will be easier to resolve, you'll feel happier more often, and your body language will immediately improve. (You'll probably even make more money.)

You've begun your journey over these past seven days, first by tuning into your own natural instincts to more accurately assess others' signals, and then by applying those lessons to your own body language. I'm going to guess that you've learned a great deal about how you can improve the communication with almost everyone in your life. Now I want you to pull all that new knowledge together and develop the attitude that's going to carry you through any situation the world throws at you, good or bad.

Before we talk about how to pull the plan into an easy-to-remember process, let's consider four aspects that I've found critical to creating the winning attitude.

Let Go of Your Need to Be Right

Research has shown that our "metaperceptions" (the ideas we have about others' ideas about us) are influenced by how our primary caregiver, usually our mom, attended to our needs through reading and acting on our baby body language. As I mentioned earlier, as babies we look at the facial expressions and gestures of our mothers to figure out who we are, and as adults we continue to do the same with other people. If other people think of us differently than our primary self-image, we'll do what we can to convince them, "No, this is who I really am" with our body language.

According to Martha Farrell Erickson, senior fellow with the Children, Youth and Family Consortium at the University of Minnesota, a child whose mom was cold and distant will duplicate that by either seeking out cold and distant relationships or acting obnoxious or withdrawn and pushing people away, thereby solidifying her self-image as unlovable. On the other hand, a child who had a consistently responsive mother will seek out good relationships and be well connected with her peers. We are constantly trying to prove that our own self-assessment is right—even at the cost of being truly loved.

I know a woman named Barbara whose mother only picked her up to feed her or change her diapers when she was a baby—that was it. Barbara is a nice person deep inside, and she can be kind and loving when she lets her guard down, but she prefers being a tough, hard-as-nails hard-ass—she *loves* having people think she's a bitch. If people are nice to her, she immediately pushes them away with cruel and mean words. As a matter of fact, she bullies her two kinder siblings for remaining in contact with the rest of their family. And you know what, at the end of the day, she gets to be right instead of admired! Lucky Barbara.

Now seriously ask yourself, "Am I stuck in a bitch-trap like Barbara?" If you are more likable than you've been letting yourself and others believe, just for today, give up the need to be right.

No matter what people have told you in the past, no matter what you've told yourself, you are amazing. You are not "shy" or "a loner" or "unmotivated." You are not "cold" or "boring" or "uncreative." You have gifts you've never even experienced before.

If you would like to stop giving your power and your confidence to someone who isn't even in your life anymore, the New Body Language can help you break those metaperception chains that have held you back in the past.

Treat Others with Respect

Whenever I ask police officers, "How many of you shake hands with the bad guys?" I'm lucky if even one out of a hundred says yes. That 1 percent, however, usually represents the officers who get thank-you notes saying things like, "Putting me in jail saved my life!" To get the same results (minus the jail part) with almost anyone, it comes down to being polite and respectful of others.

Officers who do not shake hands with suspects often find excuses ("They smell" or "They're horrible people—I don't want to touch them!"), but these are not real reasons to avoid talking to them or being polite. Everyone, even a criminal, wants to be treated with respect. The cops who shake hands often get calmer suspects and more detailed confessions.

At one of my seminars for police officers, a group from Seattle shared with me their unit's rules for dealing with suspects. The primary goals are building rapport, comfort, and respect. The three rules of this particular group of Seattle officers are:

1. Shake hands, introduce yourself, and get on a first-name basis.
2. Spend a cumulative three hours establishing rapport before discussing the crime (it does not have to be all at once, and usually isn't).
3. After rapport is established, bring the suspect along with you in your cruiser and grab some fast food for the two of you.

This may sound more like an attempt at making friends than getting suspects to confess, but it is important to note what happens on the third step: while driving around, the officer takes the suspect to a number of crime scenes, and the crime is discussed.

"We have a lot of fingerprint and DNA evidence on these crimes, but we're a bit backlogged," the officer might say. "And we know that we have you for the crime we arrested you for, as well as a couple others. But I'm sure there are more crimes you've committed that we don't know about—yet. You confess to all your crimes, I'll get the prosecuting attorney to drop several of them, and you can reduce your overall sentence. Otherwise, you can go to jail for the crime we just nabbed you on, and when you get out we'll be back in court for the others because by then our DNA and fingerprint evidence will have caught up with you."

The officer then explains the benefit to the department for confessing, which is they get to close open unsolved cases and to clean up their database. By telling the criminals what's in it for the police department, they come across as honest and sincere, and not manipulative. This strategy works over 98 percent of the time.

Everyone wants to be treated with respect, even your continually angry boss, your misunderstood teen, and your cheating ex. Keep in mind—the real root of their problems probably doesn't have anything to do with you.

Look to Help Others

I had been hired as a keynote speaker by Booz Allen Hamilton, a Fortune 500 government consulting firm, and I spoke in front of many of the company's upper management and executives. After delivering a speech and receiving a standing ovation, I headed out to the hallway. I saw Carl Salzano, the company's VP of government contract management. Next to him was an empty seat.

I kneeled down in front of him and we started talking. I shared my thoughts on how great a leader he is. It is surprising to see someone so high up in an organization acting so grounded. Carl has likable, relaxed body language, an infectious smile, an open demeanor, and is a very sociable person, yet he is a powerful leader.

At this point, he stretched out his hand and asked me to sit next to him. (My treatment of Mr. Salzano with respect through my body language and humility made it easy for him to bring me up to his level.) By treating him as the most important person in the room, I got the opportunity to build a strong rapport with him. Then again, it was easy to treat him as the most important person in the room—he was!

The two of us began to discuss the direction of my speaking career, and he invited me to come to his office for a longer discussion. Two weeks later, I met with Carl and his team during an in-house lunch. They walked me step-by-step through the process of getting government contracts. The experience was invaluable. After the meeting was over, I took Carl aside.

"What do I owe you?" I asked. "What do you want in return?"

"I only want two things," he replied. "I want you to be successful. And I want you to remain a friend of Booz Allen Hamilton."

Carl Salzano treated me as if I was the most important person in the room and provided me with priceless information that has helped me ever since.

When you treat people with respect and kindness, you will reap the rewards. Whether it's a quick resolution to a problem, a new client, or getting featured as a great person in a book (Thanks, Carl!), you will always see the benefit.

Think about your interactions with others. Is there a person you have a habit of talking down to? Try treating her like she is the most important person rather than a person whom you are forced to deal with. Doing this will not only change your body language and your relationship, it will change the way you think about life.

Someone once told me, "If you always do what you always did, you'll always get what you've always got." Changing your attitude and body language can open great new doors for you and improve your life in ways you might have never thought possible.

Don't Wait for Happiness

People who have negative beliefs about themselves *do* have the skills necessary to deal with their problems—but because of their negative attitude, they avoid solving the problems and get trapped in a world of constant worry and fear. Worriers are not in worse situations than those who don't worry; it is simply the worrier's point of reference to problems that causes his or her misery. When something feels bad, it can impair the person's ability to solve problems.

When we fret and worry about what could happen, we stall our happiness. Instead of living in this moment, enjoying what it has to offer, we push it away in favor of a threatening future that hasn't even shown up yet. Putting our lives on hold until that next major life change— "just as soon as I lose weight/get out of debt/buy my first house/get a promotion and raise"—will actually do little to boost our overall happiness. We must not wait to be happy. We have to start right now, right this very second.

Putting It All Together

The final phase of mastering the New Body Language is to move from the passenger's seat of your life to behind the wheel. I've been in the driver's seat for most of this book, but now it's your turn. When you're out on the road and looking for a thruway to get you where you're going, take out the the 7-Day plan and let it be your road map to success.

▶ *The Rearview Mirror—The Old Body Language.* You can't move forward if you're constantly looking back. While some people are stuck believing in the myths of the Old Body Language (mind reading, judging others without asking Powerful Questions, and being confused about what move to use when) you know the secret to moving forward, it's the new body language: Accuracy + Application + Attitude = Success.

▶ *The Gas Gauge—Baselining.* If you don't check how much gas you have before your journey, you could get stranded. You always need to calibrate or gauge others' baseline behavior before you add meaning to any of their nonverbals.

▶ *Your Seat Belt—The Belly Button Rule.* The seat belt locks your belly button into place, which is straight ahead, facing your target and where you want to go. We face our belly button toward people we like, admire, and trust, and we use it as a barometer of where we want to go. Use your "navel intelligence" and point your belly button toward the most important person in the room, or the person you want to influence positively, especially when you shake his or her hand. The last thing you want to do is unintentionally give someone of importance the "cold shoulder."

▶ *The Heater (or Air Conditioner)—Workin' the Naughty Bits and Other Lower Extremities.* External conditions can make driving difficult at times. For instance, when we're cold, we shrink up to warm up. And when we're warm, we spread out, take up space, and relax. During times of social discomfort, be sure to check how your emotional temperature is affecting your naughty bits and legs. If you want to disappear and go unnoticed, close up and take up less space (fold your hands in the fig leaf position and keep your feet less than six inches apart). But if you want to be noticed and appear self-assured and confident, widen your stance to six to ten inches and keep your "bits" open (hands at sides, on hips, or behind back), and you'll send the message that you're not a pushover.

▶ *Side Mirrors—The Right Side Rule.* Driving is about judgment and awareness. If you don't check your blind spots, you could put yourself in a dangerous situation. Discovering your own and others' good and bad sides is no different. Next time someone is irritated by you or you want to get the upper hand, use good judgment and get on *their* good side. But if your nerves are getting the best of you, put on your blinker, subtly change lanes, and put them on *your* good side!

▶ *Hit the Horn—Power Gestures.* The horn's primary purpose is to get someone's attention. It's our power gesture behind the wheel. Power gestures like the palm-down gesture, hands on the hips, subtle touches, and all of the steeples will definitely help you get noticed and respected. Just be careful not to combine too many dominant moves at once and abuse your power, like those road ragers.

▶ *Crack in Your Windshield—The Dangerous Four (Emotions).* The tiny cracks we get when a small rock hits our windshield resemble the fleeting microexpressions on a person's face. If we don't address them immediately, they could turn into a bigger problem. For instance, an unhappy employee who fakes happiness might not be returning customer calls or could be disrespectful on the phone. Or a scared teenager who pretends to be angry all the time might really be depressed and suicidal. A loving spouse may be leaking contempt because he's been having an affair for years with your best friend and he thinks you don't have a clue. When you spot any of the Dangerous Four, tread lightly, and when it's safe, ask Powerful Questions to get to the truth behind the hidden emotion.

▶ *The GPS—The QWQ Formula.* When you enter four items of your destination address (state, city, street, number of street) into a GPS, you receive a whole lot of information back. Instead of attempting to be a mind reader, when you ask Powerful Questions, you'll get more information than you might expect. When you reach a detour in your relationships or an inevitable speed bump, initiate the QWQ: Question, W.A.I.T. (Why Am I Talking?, aka say nothing until they speak), Question and you won't have to hold on to your seat for a bumpy ride; instead you'll smoothly navigate through life.

▶ *The Ignition Key—Putting It All Together (Attitude).* It doesn't matter if your car passed the safety inspection and the emission test, that it's full of gas and in great shape—those things won't help you get to your destination without the car key. Without the key your car will remain motionless and stuck in your driveway. The key to the New Body Language is your attitude. It's the must-have ingredient to all success. Without the key the car won't run; without the right attitude, you'll never get what you want.

All Together, Now: New Attitude Postprogram Exercises

You've completed the 7-Day program, and you've learned a lot about how to channel your natural instincts for body language into an attitude that will win many new fans. To help you put the finishing touches on your own makeover, do these final exercises. They'll help you take a good look at where you stand now, and how you can tackle any remaining obstacles between you and your dreams.

▶ *Reframe the Problem.* At a conference, a fellow speaker called on me in the audience and asked, "Janine, if the World Trade Center was still standing and I connected a two-by-four from the top of Tower One to the top of Tower Two and put a million dollars out in the middle of the board, would you crawl out to get it?"

Having worked in the World Trade Center as a public information officer with ATF a decade earlier, I was familiar with the raw power of the wind at the top of the Towers. Without hesitation, I replied, "No!"

Then he gave me the same scenario, but put Angus out there sitting dead center on the two-by-four. Again he asked, "Would you go out there now?"

As you can imagine, I barely held back tears, picturing little eight-month-old Angus out on that board all by himself, over thirteen hundred feet in the air. "Yes! I would go get him!" I confidently shouted. Wouldn't you, if it were the person *you* loved more than anyone else on this planet?

The way you define a problem often brings the solution. Sometimes, to take action we need to change our perspective. Ask yourself, "Am I doing what I have to do to have a life of abundance and success?" Think about it. Even if your heart races and your hands shake, change your perspective and do the thing you fear most anyway—it just might be good for your soul.

In your journal, jot down a couple of notes:

How have you been defining the challenges in your life?

How would your body language and your life be different if you were to look at them from a new perspective?

What if you looked at your mother-in-law problem as you would a problem with money, a friend, or a hobby?

What if you looked at your dating problem as you would a challenge at work—or even a life and death issue?

What different courses of action might you take in these situations instead because of this new perspective?

▶ *Break Limiting Beliefs.* Occasionally do you say to yourself, "I'm not good enough," "I'm not lovable," "I'll never win, so why try?" "I'm shy," "People don't care what I have to say," or something similar? If so, you have created a belief that limits you from expressing yourself fully and stops you from showing up for others as the truly wonderful, whole, and complete person you already are.

Limiting beliefs are repetitive unhelpful thoughts that are tied in with self-esteem and involve our perceptions of the world. Eventually, these limiting beliefs, such as uncertainty, defiance, and nervousness, become true for us. Then our body language suffers and we unintentionally leak powerful evidence of our insecurities to the world. Do this instead:

1. Write down seven beliefs that you have about yourself and the world around you.
2. Ask yourself which of these beliefs are still useful to you. Put a check mark or a smiley face next to the beliefs that add value and help you have a life that you love.
3. Circle the beliefs that are holding you back; these are your limiting beliefs. For each of your limiting beliefs, write down what might be possible instead.
4. If these new possibilities were true, how would it change your body language? How would you show up for others?

Once you are able to identify your limiting beliefs you can break through your self-sabotaging thoughts. And an extraordinary transformation will occur, first internally with your thought patterns, then externally with your posture, stance, hand gestures, facial expressions, and voice tone and pitch.

▶ *Give Up the Need to Be Right Today.* I know this exercise might just kill a couple of you—it's torturous for me to do, that's for sure—but just for today let everyone else think they're right. Don't be smug about it, be sincere. Even say to people, "You're right." When someone says it's going to rain, but it's sunny, respond, "You're right." Notice what this does to the conversation, how it changes the energy of the situation. Think about how that might help you in other situations or other relationships.

▶ *Fail Your Way to Success.* That's right, failure can actually boost your confidence.

A study was done of pottery students. One section of the class was told, "You have to make this pot perfectly. You get one chance."

The other side of the class was told, "You get to make a pot, but you get to fail as many times as you want. You don't have to make a perfect pot. You just make a pot."

At the end of the process, the side that got to fail was the side that created nearly flawless pots.

We think we've got to do everything at once to succeed. We don't have to. Failure is absolutely beneficial, as long as you don't allow it to overwhelm you. Think back on some of your failures and gain confidence. Let it remind you what you're not doing anymore—you're not living that way anymore and you're not repeating the same mistakes again. But if you had not failed, you would not know what to avoid or perhaps what to pursue.

▶ *Change Your Focus.* Focus on things that empower you, and you will find it impossible to concentrate on your limiting beliefs at the same time. This means that when we truly concentrate on what's working in our lives, our minds block out what's not working. For instance, when you ask yourself, "What am I grateful for?" Your mind will direct its thinking to answering the question, which will automatically change your feelings as well. This exercise requires you to frame your current experiences in a positive light, challenge yourself to be unreasonable, and take action even in the face of fear.

Ask yourself the following questions:

How do I want to feel?
How can I have fun doing the things I need to do today?
What am I grateful for?
What are my favorite memories?
How could my life be transformed if I did this thing I fear?
How does this problem or challenge create a new opportunity?
What actions can I—or must I—take to transform this situation?
How can I contribute to other people's lives?

TEN

The Final Word: Finding Garcia

> Most people are like a falling leaf that
> drifts and turns in the air, flutters, and
> falls to the ground. But a few others are
> like stars which travel on one defined
> path: no wind reaches them, they have
> within themselves their guide and path.
> —HERMAN HESSE (1877-1962), Siddhartha

In the late 1800s, President William McKinley abruptly met with the head of the Bureau of Military Intelligence for the United States. The United States had decided to support Cuba's fight for independence from Spain, and cooperation between the rebel forces in Cuba and the United States would be crucial if the mission were to be a success. McKinley needed to find a self-reliant soldier who could get a message to the leader of the rebels, General Garcia. Although no one knew Garcia's exact location, they believed he was leading the rebel troops somewhere in the mountains of Cuba.

The president called upon a young soldier named Rowan to get a message to Garcia. The soldier was told to get a message to the leader of the rebels, who would be found somewhere in the eastern part of Cuba. And he was told that this task belonged to him and him alone. Without asking, "What does he look like?" "Do you have a picture of him?" "Who was he last in contact with?" "How can I get there?" "What should I wear?" "I have plans this weekend, can I do it on Monday?" the soldier took the order, created an action plan, and found Garcia.

Name: David Croushore
Age: 24
Occupation: Research Assistant at the
Federal Reserve

What was holding you back? I am a passionate and competitive person. I love to argue with friends and coworkers, and I'll take bets on just about anything. Despite my reckless nature, I was quiet and reserved around people I didn't know. I tried to live my life by being open to all outcomes yet attached to none and accepting all invitations.

My friends had different theories. One said I didn't take enough risks socially and that I put too much pressure on myself. Another said I'm very emotionally driven and I change my mind as my emotions change. Another said I don't dedicate myself to one task enough and I let distractions get in the way of success. I planned on applying to graduate schools in the near future, so I thought that having better body language could help me in interviews.

How have you changed? Since going through Janine's program I've developed an understanding of myself that makes me much more confident in my opinions and ideas. Without having to worry about how I was being seen by others, I've been able to open up and share a lot of my own knowledge more freely. I've gained a new circle of friends to complement my old ones. I have a definite direction and purpose, which brings a lot of joy to my life.

"Finding Garcia" really changed my life. It's easy to take the passive approach, to sit back and wait to see what happens to us. The lesson we can learn from "Finding Garcia" is that we need to be proactive. Instead of letting life happen to us, we need to make it happen *for* us.

I used to assume that if I just went with the flow, I'd end up with the right woman. But a couple months after learning to be proactive, I met the girl of my dreams. She, like me, was always busy with her own life, and we easily could have drifted apart. However, with the "Finding Garcia" lesson in mind, I took the initiative and actively pursued a deeper relationship. We're now engaged and I can't imagine my life without her. All it took was one change in my outlook to make it happen.

Now, several months later, I've completed a triathlon and I have a new job, making 40 percent more than I used to. Janine's program was the catalyst that made this all possible.

A Message to Garcia

In 1899, a man by the name of Elbert Hubbard wrote a brief article about Rowan that has since become one of the most published documents in the history of the printed word. *A Message to Garcia* has been translated into every major language on earth and has been published as a stand-alone volume, one of the strongest-selling books of all time.

This little story is about self-reliance, determination, and perseverance. Could you get a message to Garcia without asking a single question? You could if you were desperate to succeed.

If your life was on the line and failure wasn't an option, you would find a way, wouldn't you? You wouldn't settle for average and you wouldn't constantly tell yourself and others, "I could never be as confident as you. It's just not in me." Instead, you would list all the reasons why you couldn't do it, and then you would find a way to do it anyway. You would stop waiting for someone else to control your destiny and you would choose success, right? You would choose to live.

In the weeks and months to come, while continuing on your journey to using the New Body Language to get what you want, remember to check in with yourself each week to see how your progress is coming. Look at where you are and see if you've veered off course on the way to achieving your intended goals. Pilots know this lesson well. Due to turbulence, clouds, wind, rain, a flock of birds, the curvature of the earth, and other factors, they veer off their flight plan nearly 75 percent of the time.

Have you ever set goals and taken steps to reach those goals, only to have an outside force, perhaps people in your life who do not know where *they* are going or what *they* want, attempt to derail *your* success? The way to stay on course to achieving a more confident, happier, and more satisfied life is to be flexible, adaptable, and unstoppable. Think about it, does the pilot who veers off course say to herself, "Well, this plan didn't work exactly the way it was supposed to—I give up. I'll plop the plane down right here." No! Pilots adjust their plan until they find an adaptable solution that will get them to their intended destination. The same holds true with your goals and plans: be flexible and adapt the lessons learned throughout this program. Add a splash of being unstoppable, and you'll be well on your way to landing what you want in your life.

Now that you have completed the 7-day plan on using the New Body Language to get what you want, go out and get it!

You have everything you need. You are whole and complete exactly as you are—stop waiting and go find your Garcia!

Now, I am going to ask you some Powerful Questions.

You now know when your body language either helps or hurts your message, right?

You know how to portray confidence and authority, and know what moves make you disappear, correct?

And wouldn't you agree that you now notice when others deviate from their baseline behavior? And you know how to ask Powerful Questions to peel away the different layers of communication, right?

And if your life depended on it, you could find Garcia, right?

My book landed in *your* hands for a reason, and I'm so grateful it did. I hope one day our paths cross in person. In the meantime, remember, *You Say More Than You Think,* so sit up straight, relax your body, and subtly smile because you now have all the skills you need to adapt and make work what might not be working right away for you—in any situation!

I believe in you.

Now, go get 'em! Go find Garcia, baby!

The Body Reader: 7-Second Fixes for Any Situation

You're armed with all the tools you need, you've got the basics down cold, and you've moved on to the advanced techniques. Now how about a quick-and-dirty cheat sheet for those situations when you just need one trick to turn things in your favor? Unless losing suits you, seven seconds is all you need to carry out your New Body Language–based operation and swing any awkward encounter in your favor. Check it out.

Your New Coworker is Confident and You Want to Build Rapport Fast

Their Move	Your Move

Do This: Keep your three power zones—neck dimple, belly button, and naughty bits—open and relax your arms.

Get This: Exude cool confidence and the person you are meeting with will quickly see you as an equal.

You're Overworked, Your Child Misbehaved, and You're Scaring Him

Their Move	Your Move

Do This: Get down to his level and use an open-palm gesture.

Get This: Still come across as authoritative, but maintain respect for your child.

You're Coming on Too Strong for Her!

Their Move	Your Move

Do This: Become smaller by closing your stance to no more than six inches and create a wall by holding your glass in front of you. And slightly angle your belly button away from your new gal pal.

Get This: Become less aggressive, increase your mystery quotient, and gain more time to win her over.

He's Too into Himself and You Want to Disappear Fast!

Their Move	Your Move

 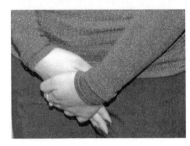

Do This: Stand in the fig leaf position, or if seated, cross your leg closest to the person and create a wall—and be sure to look away. The trick to becoming invisible is to become small.

Get This: Decrease your visibility by making his target smaller. You can also de-escalate an argument or confrontation this way. You'll still seem likable, but you'll silently send him packing.

You're Both Hot and Single, But No One Is Approaching

Their Move	Your Move

Do This: Open up the center of your body, and angle your belly buttons away from the bar and toward the center of the room.

Get This: Increase your confidence signals and become approachable. Immediately, you'll let the fellas know that you're both open for conversation (and maybe a drink!).

You Want to Get the Girl, But You're Not Having Any Luck

Their Move	Your Move

Do This: Move the chairs, which will move your bodies, and sit to her side instead of directly across from her.

Get This: Minimize a confrontational position, increase your likability, enhance rapport, and move the girl enough to get her number!

You're Deathly Shy and You're on *Her* Bad Side

Their Move	Your Move

Do This: Keep the hottie on *your* good side.

Get This: Decrease your internal negative thinking and nerves, and gain a splash of self-confidence, before moving to her good side.

Let the Big Boys Know You Can Play Hardball Too!

Their Move	Your Move

Do This: Bring out the godfather steeple, also called the high steeple. If he matches your godfather, then steeple wider and higher.

Get This: Decrease his impact and power, and increase your authority, power, and confidence. You're showing him that you can play with the big boys, and you're sure of what you're saying—you have a plan.

You Screwed Up and He's Not Happy

Their Move	Your Move

Do This: When you shake hands give *him* the upper hand by facing your palm up, which will force him into the power palm-down position. Say, "I'm sorry [say name]." Then acknowledge the damage or hurt. "There's no excuse. It won't happen again. Please forgive me."

Get This: Stop a communication breakdown, increase forgivability, and build integrity and trust. You'll also validate his feelings, decrease his grudge, feed his ego, and ultimately lessen the blow on you!

Dealing with a Coworker Who's a Jerk

Their Move	Your Move

Do This: Bring out the heavy artillery and fire off the handgun steeple.

Get This: Decrease his power, increase your authority and personal power, and ultimately gain control over the conversation.

Dealing with a Domineering Subordinate

Their Move	Your Move

Do This: Stand up and stretch, then continue the conversation from the standing position while you escort the person out of your office.

Get This: Whether the person likes it or not, you'll remind him that you are the boss and you are in charge of him!

BONUS BARRIER BUSTER: If the subordinate still tries to dominate you, invade his space: Sit in his chair, put your feet on his desk, and make a call from his phone—in perfect time for him to walk in and see.

Dominate the Office Bitch!

Their Move	Your Move

Do This: Immediately stand up over the handgun steepler, and point out something on a piece of paper in front of her or on the board. Then stay standing. DO NOT RETREAT!

Get This: Increase your confidence, authority, clout, and control, while you decrease her power. Boo-ya!

Stop a Pushy Saleswoman in Her Tracks

Their Move	Your Move

Do This: Lean one hand against a wall, bend one knee, and take up as much space as possible, put your other hand hooked from your belt or pocket (highlighting your bits), or if you're sitting take up as much space as humanly possible.

Get This: It's as if you have gotten there earlier and peed in the perimeter; yes, you mark your territory and send the message that you can't be taken advantage of, or influenced easily.

You Want to Make the BEST First Impression on Your Job Interview, But You're Too Far Away!

Their Move	Your Move

Do This: Ask if you can show the interviewer something, for example, your portfolio or something mentioned in the company brochure. Stand up and show her the item. Before sitting back down, casually move your chair, so you are slightly diagonal from the interviewer—on her good side. Slightly lean forward, open your center line, make sure both of your hands can be seen, and touch her desk.

Get This: Your favorite crossed leg and hand to your face are no longer creating a massive barrier. You'll avoid looking judgmental, disconnected, or even deceptive, and you'll immediately increase your face value, which will increase your odds of getting the job.

Create Your Own Body Language Power Team

How do we bring the New Body Language into the lives of the people in our world? How do we teach our fellow book club members, friends, family, coworkers, or employees to see and appreciate its value without overwhelming them? How do we encourage them to understand the importance of reading others' nonverbals and adapting their own body language to boost poise, confidence, and results? If you're looking to establish a playful environment that fosters collaborative teamwork to solve problems, and inspire and lift others to reach abundance, success, and endless opportunities in their lives, here's your chance to create your own Body Language Power Team (BLPT)!

Being a part of a BLPT is an exciting experience. Creating a BLPT is just as exciting, but takes a bit more work, coordination, and cooperation. The time spent at each BLPT event is less about learning facts than about application and integration of the success strategies of the plan highlighted throughout this book.

Creating the right type of BLPT for your group or organization can be a challenge, but all the needed forms for setting up your Body Language Power Team (BLPT) are posted for *free* on www.yousay morethanyouthink.com.

BODY LANGUAGE POWER TEAM
CERTIFIED FACILITATORS

Many of my former BLPT members, some of whom are highlighted throughout this book, are now BLPT facilitators, who lead and guide teams of people from around the globe on how to most effectively implement the premises of the 7-Day plan. Sometimes they'll be right there with you in person, and other times they'll meet with you and your team over the computer or over the phone. If you're interested in joining a BLPT team in your area that's facilitated by a certified Body Language Power Team leader, visit www.yousaymorethanyouthink.com to sign up today!

SELECTED
REFERENCES

Aaronson, L. "Dress Like a Winner." *Psychology Today*, March/April 2005.

———. "Friends Don't Pick Up on Anger." *Psychology Today*, May/June 2005.

Anthes, E. "Six Ways to Boost Brainpower." *Scientific American Mind*, February 2009.

DiVesta, F. J. and D. A. Smith. "The Pausing Principle: Increasing the Efficiency of Memory for Ongoing Events." *Contemporary Educational Psychology* 4 (1979): 288–96.

Flora, C. "Metaperceptions: How Do You See Yourself?" *Psychology Today*, May/June 2005.

Friedman, R. and A. J. Elliot. "The Effect of Arm Crossing on Persistence and Performance." *European Journal of Social Psychology* 38, no. 3 (2008): 449–61.

Goldin-Meadow, S., et al. "Gesturing Gives Children New Ideas about Math." *Psychological Science* 20, no. 3 (2009): 267–72.

Harrigan, J. A. and R. Rosenthal. "Physicians' Head and Body Positions as Determinants of Perceived Rapport." *Journal of Applied Social Psychology* 13, no. 6 (2003): 496–509.

Harris, M. "Rich Too Posh for Eye Contact: Study: Body Language Tips Off Your Status." *Calgary Herald*, February 7, 2009.

Hicklin, L. A., C. Ryan, D. K. Wong, and A. E. Hinton. "Nose-Bleeds after Sildenafil (Viagra)." *Journal of the Royal Society of Medicine* 95, no. 8 (2002): 402–40.

James, W. T. "A Study of the Expression of Bodily Posture." *Journal of General Psychology* 7 (1932): 405–37.

Kelly, S. D., C. Kravitz, and M. Hopkins. "Neural Correlates of Bimodal Speech and Gesture Comprehension." *Brain and Language* 89, no. 1 (2004): 253–60.

Kraus, M. W. and D. Keltner. "Signs of Socioeconomic Status: A Thin-Slicing Approach." *Psychological Science* 20, no. 1 (2009): 99–106 (8).

Mehrabian, A. "Inference of Attitude from the Posture, Orientation, and Distance of a Communicator." *Journal of Consulting and Clinical Psychology* 32 (1968): 296–308.

Nicholson, C. "Olympic Gold Medal: Is the Body Language of Triumph (or Defeat) Biological?" *Scientific American*, August 11, 2008.

Rowe, M. L. and S. Goldin-Meadow. "Differences in Early Gesture Explain SES Disparities in Child Vocabulary Size at School Entry." *Science* 323, no. 5916 (2009): 951–53.

Schnall, S. and J. D. Laird. "Keep Smiling: Enduring Effects of Facial Expressions and Postures on Emotional Experience and Memory." *Cognition and Emotion* 17, no. 5 (2003): 787–97.

Tracy, J. L. and D. Matsumoto. "The Spontaneous Expression of Pride and Shame: Evidence for Biologically Innate Nonverbal Displays." *Proceedings of the National Academy of Sciences* 105, no. 33 (2008): 11655–60.

Wachsmuth, I. "Gestures Offer Insight." *Scientific American Mind*, October 4, 2006.

Walsh, B. "Study: Babies Who Gesture Learn Words Sooner." Time.com, February 12, 2009.

Thanks to all the extraordinary people who made this book possible: Thank you to my amazingly strategic and tremendously talented literary agent, Dan Lazar (and his imaginary coffee table); my super-organized and unstoppable manager, Traci Allen; my new princess-worthy senior research consultant, Jerusalem Merkebu; and my numerous interns who every day believe in me and support my personal mission to educate the world on The New Body Language.

Thank you to my editor-extraordinaire, Heather Jackson of Crown, who told me that I was already a "butterfly," sent me a $40,000 e-mail, and who took a wild all-over-the-place book proposal and, as she does with every book she touches, turned it into rock-solid platinum—she's an author's dream come true! And thanks to the rest of my Crown team for their unrelenting awesomeness: Annsley Rosner, Katie Wainwright, Sara Breivogel, Amy Boorstein, Terry Deal, Linnea Knollmueller, Elizabeth Rendfleisch, Jennifer O'Connor, Mary Choteborsky, Patty Berg, Linda Kaplan, Jill Flaxman, Emily Timberlake, and to anyone else at Crown who in one way or another touched this book and made it better; and the biggest hug in the world is saved for the beautiful and graceful Tina Constable for keeping the offer on the table, taking me back, and providing me the incredible honor to work with Heather; thank you, thank you, THANK YOU!

And a tall order of gratitude goes out to my fabulous cowriter, Mariska van Aalst (and her snazzy new haircut that has yet to be seen), who with class, an unstoppable drive, and a huge heart was able to take my ADD writing binges, sew them together, and create this amazing bestselling book—she's a creative genius. To my favorite college professor, Harris Elder, who in 1988 cleverly pushed my limits when he had our entire Comp 101 class read the *New Yorker* magazine each week, and who exactly two decades later, from page one of this book tirelessly copyedited every sentence before I sent it to my cowriter. His support, encouragement, and guidance have forever changed the course of my life.

Thank you to all the members of my ATF and law enforcement family who have touched, moved, and inspired me in so many ways. In particular, my mentors J. J. Newberry, Neal Earl, Susan (McCarron) Boyd, and Theresa Stoop without whose professional guidance, support, and generosity this book literally would not be possible; and my deepest gratitude and love also go out to my ATF sister and confidant, Myisha Wallace, thank you for your constant love and support and for spending your entire Sunday logging in ninety-five pictures into a spreadsheet, YOU ROCK! And a gigantic thanks to Sissy Bray, Ben Peeters, Wayne Bettencourt, Angela Long, Chuck Turner, Jimmy Ebert, Tom Shalayda, Regina Domingo, Joe Bradley, Jennifer Dollan-Mossor, Peggy Elmore, Nick Colucci, Jeff Reed, Guy Thomas, Ken Chisholm, Edgar Domenech, Tom Murray, Judy LeDoux, Clarence Lawrence, Chris Demline, Marcia Lambert, James Cavanaugh, Lynne Dement, John Torres, Ray Torres, Steve Bisnett, Tina Atkins, Wanda Outlaw, Geneva Dunaway, Mark Logan, Larry Ford, Sandra Thompson, Audrey Stucko, Lee Vannett, Angelo Vara, Kim Allen, Jeffrey Bell, Jeff Cohen, John Daffron, and Charlie Humphrey and his missing white gym socks. Also, much appreciation and admiration goes out to the entire elite force of detecting deception expert instructors from the Institute of Analytic Interviewing, including the detecting deception research master Dr. Maureen O'Sullivan.

I'd also like to extend my deep appreciation to all the media personalities and current and former incredibly talented producers, writers, and editors, who have given me much more than fifteen minutes of fame. You have given me an amazing platform to help struggling men and women gain an edge in the game of life. From the bottom of my heart, thank you especially to those from the world's favorite magazine *Cosmopolitan:* Super editor in chief Kate White, and editors extraordinaire Ky Henderson, Bethany Heitman, Molly Triffin, Holly Eagleson, and Mina Azodi; and from NBC's *Today* show and *Weekend Today:* Al Roker, Ann Curry, Natalie Morales, Hoda Kotb, Lester Holt, Jenna Wolfe, Amy Robach, Marc Victor, Michele Leone, Michelle Fanucci, Sara Haines, Don Nash, Sara Pines, Robert Ciridon, Gil Reisfield, Lindsay Sobel, Dan Barbossa, Emily Goldberg, Matt Zimmerman, Kim Cornett, Eric Jackson, and Deb from wardrobe for always making me look my best. And I have to send a big thanks to the one and only charismatic, dimple flashing, Donny Deutsch; the fabulous Mary Duffy; the smart and savvy Larry King; the late Tony Snow (where I made my media debut on FOX News—I miss you, Tony); and two of my favorite TV producers on the planet, Scott Eason and Marianne Schaberg. Thank you to the likable TV cook Rachael Ray for sitting on my lap on national TV and gaining the attention of my future literary agent, which ultimately led to this book—you and your EVOO totally ROCK THE HOUSE, girl! A big thanks to the *Rachael Ray Show*'s behind-the-scenes stage magician, Vita, and super-producer Meredith Weintraub, and the ever wonderful producer Maggie Barnes, and my unsuspecting body language analysis makeovers Nicole Nelson and Julianne. More thanks go out to CNN's Matt Hibbeln; FOX News' Joshua McCarroll, Greg Gutfeld, and Greta Van Susteren; *The Washington Post*'s Dan Zak; *The New York Times*' Katie Thomas; and *USA Today*'s Lorena Blas.

Thanks to *Queer Eye for the Straight Guy*'s Ted Allen for instructing me in the Green Room at the *Today* show to never say the word "groin" on national television again, instead to call it "The Naughty Bits," I owe you a drink and a big hug! Thanks to the very funny and super friendly Cloris Leachman and her beautiful and talented granddaughter, Skye Englund—that was one dinner that I will always remember.

A big pat on the back also to my photographers, Freddie Liberman and Peter Stepanek. You guys did such an amazing job and this book is better because of you both. A huge hug and kiss to Todd Shoemaker for videotaping and extraordinarily editing the Body Language Power Teams (BLPT) seven-day journeys; you are totally destined for greatness, my talented new friend (check out the BLPT footage at www. yousaymorethanyouthink.com). Additional thanks and appreciation goes out to my new friend and fellow author and speaker. Thanks for your endless positivity and prayers; I'm your new biggest fan. Thank you to Michael Carlan and his exceptional special events company for young professionals, www.prosinthecity.com. Massive gratitude also travels Northwest to Victoria, Canada, directly in the hands and heart of my superstar web designer, Nicole Lamac (and her team of experts, Chuckie and Aaron, and to her hubby, Radko, who has a knack for making me laugh). And much appreciation and love goes out to all my friends, fellow authors and speakers, and clients, especially, my BFF #1, who has always had my back, the one-and-only Terry Moore (you are literally the funniest human being I have ever met in my life—you belong on *Mad TV*), the creative and loving Tamia Sheldon, Erin Casey and family, all the O'Neils (especially smart and courageous little Eddie, my future VP), Pat and Jim McCue, Elaine McNeil, Kristen Colleran, Carl Salzano, Ali Nichols, Jacqueline Whitmore, John Christensen, Dale Atkins, Debra Fine, Ed Buice, Frank Marsh, Kevin Morison, the AOL Wonder Women, my favorite "Chicks on Wine," (Lisa, Lisa, and Kristina), Kandi Haupt, Jeanna Callahan, Mary Carmen Cordoba, Ashley Sandberg, Alkies Lapas, Mel Robbins, Tom and Meg Stewart (and Meg's mom), Melanie Coffin, Em Cambell, Beckie Cattie, and the best comedy coach in the country, Tim Davis. And to all my BLI instructors—Niki Boone, Dr. Susan Miller, Michele Pollard Patrick, Stephen Facella, and Aaron Brehove.

Last, but not least, thank you to my extraordinary parents, Lorraine and Charlie Driver, for experientially sharing with me the true ingredients to ridiculous amounts of success: from Mom's unwavering positive thinking and determination to graduate from nursing school (top of her class) while successfully raising three small kids at home, to later getting her master's in education, to her brilliant mantra when she worked with the elderly homeless, "As the Kenny Rogers song goes, I know when to hold 'em and I know when to fold 'em, I know when to walk away. Except, I never walk away, I just come in from a different angle!"; to Dad's unwavering dependability and meticulous attention to detail while working two jobs for over forty years, to all the free oil changes a daughter could need, to not letting go of Neil because he gave his word he'd hold on, to his success motto, "Do it right the first time or don't do it at all!" You are much more than the wind beneath my wings, you are the two people I admire and look up to the most. I'm so grateful that God chose you to be *my* parents. Thanks, too, to my husband, Leif Larson, for always making me laugh and for lending me your right brain cells when I was stuck on a word while I was writing—you are a creative mastermind, I love you; my son, Angus, for your big push-me-over-style hugs, sweet kisses, and songs and tales about dinosaurs, baby snakes, and wild animal kingdoms (I love you and your i-m-a-g-i-n-a-t-i-o-n); and thanks to my wicked awesome and beautiful sisters Kerry Strollo and Caileen Horrigan and their husbands Dan Strollo and Michael Horrigan and their beautiful children (Deirdre, Bella, Jake, Tommy, Ellie, Abigail, and new baby Brooke) for always being my front-row cheerleaders and telling me that each time I'm on the *Today* show that I look better and performed better than the last (even when it's not always true). I love you all up to the moon and down to the pipes, and I would do anything on this earth to keep you all safe, happy, and loved.

Enough said?!

INDEX

ABOUT THE AUTHOR

JANINE DRIVER is the CEO of The Body Language Institute (www. bodylanguageinstitute.com), an exclusive certification program that provides companies the fastest way to save time and make money. She is also an international trainer and keynote speaker who playfully provides salespeople, professionals, and executives with cutting-edge, scientifically based communication tools on how to win new business, increase sales, improve selection of salespeople and sales managers, and generate a significant return on investment. Janine is a popular media guest who has made appearances on NBC's *Today*, *The Rachael Ray Show*, and CNN's *Larry King Live*. She has been quoted in the *New York Times*, the *Washington Post*, and in magazines such as *Cosmopolitan* and *Psychology Today*. Janine spent fifteen years as a federal law enforcement officer within the United States Department of Justice. Janine lives in Alexandria, Virginia, with her husband and son.

To take your FREE online body language mini-course or to book Janine for your next event, she invites you to visit www.yousaymore thanyouthink.com today.

A percentage of all author profits from this book will be donated to the Susan G. Komen Breast Cancer Foundation (www.komen.org), which is dedicated to education and research about causes, treatment, and the search for a cure.